Ruth Bader Ginsburg

In Her Own Words

D1010169

Ruth Bader Ginsburg
In Her Own Words

EDITED BY
Helena Hunt

AN AGATE IMPRINT

CHICAGO

Printed in the United States of America

Library of Congress Cataloging-in-Publication Data

Names: Ginsburg, Ruth Bader, author. | Hunt, Helena, editor.
Title: Ruth Bader Ginsburg : in her own words / Edited by Helena Hunt.
Description: Chicago : B2 Books, 2018. | Includes bibliographical references and index.
Identifiers: LCCN 2017059985 (print) | LCCN 2017060217 (ebook) | ISBN 9781572848184 (ebook) | ISBN 1572848189 (ebook) | ISBN 9781572842496 (pbk. : alk. paper) | ISBN 1572842490 (pbk. : alk. paper)
Subjects: LCSH: Ginsburg, Ruth Bader. | Women judges--United States. | Women lawyers--United States. | United States. Supreme Court.
Classification: LCC KF8745.G56 (ebook) | LCC KF8745.G56 G56 2018 (print) | DDC 349.73--dc23
LC record available at https://lccn.loc.gov/2017059985

First printing: April 2018

10 9 8 7 6 5 4   19 20 21 22

B2 Books is an imprint of Agate Publishing. Agate books are available in bulk at discount prices. For more information, go to agatepublishing.com.

I think the simplest explanation and one that captures the idea [of feminism], is the song that Marlo Thomas sang, "Free to Be You and Me." Free to be, if you were a girl, doctor, lawyer, Indian chief, anything you wanted to be. And if you were a boy, and you like teaching, you like nursing, you would like to have a doll, that's OK too. [Feminism is] that notion that we should each be free to develop our own talents, whatever they may be, and not be held back by artificial barriers—man-made barriers, certainly not heaven-sent.

—RUTH BADER GINSBURG

Contents

Introduction

J USTICE RUTH BADER GINSBURG deserves all the notoriety she gets. Both men and women have benefited enormously from her decades of advocacy for equal rights for all people, regardless of sex, income, race, or any of the other accidents of birth that have historically tended to determine one's status in US society. From Brooklyn to the bench, she has left a big footprint for someone who stands just over five feet tall.

Joan Ruth Bader (her name was later changed to distinguish her from other girls named Joan in school) was born in Brooklyn in 1933, the daughter and granddaughter of Jewish immigrants to the United States. Under her mother's encouragement—and discipline—she excelled in school and became an avid reader, talents that led her to Cornell upon her high school graduation.

Ginsburg's mother, Celia Bader, though she died the day before her daughter graduated from high school, had a lasting influence on Ginsburg's life and work. Ginsburg often says that her mother was the most intelligent person she ever knew, and that if she had had the opportunity, she could have accomplished as much as Ginsburg herself eventually would. Throughout her life, Ginsburg has worked to ensure that women like her mother are not limited by their sex and have all the access to education, work, and success that men do.

At Cornell, chosen by her family in part because it promised an advantageous marriage (in the 1950s, the school enrolled four male students for every woman),

Ginsburg again proved her academic potential—and began what would become one of the most distinguished law careers of the 20th century. One of her professors, Robert E. Cushman, called to his students' attention the injustices being done against US citizens by Joseph McCarthy and the House Un-American Activities Committee, which at the time was conducting controversial investigations into Communist activities in the United States. Cushman openly admired the lawyers who represented those brought before the committee and defended the rights of US citizens to think and speak freely without fear of government interference. Those lawyers showed Ginsburg the potential of a life in the law, and it was their influence she followed throughout her career in defending the rights of ordinary citizens.

In addition to graduating with honors and a Phi Beta Kappa membership, Ginsburg also found what her family wanted for her—a husband. But Martin Ginsburg wasn't, as Ginsburg herself says, the typical male undergraduate of the 1950s. He admired Ginsburg's intelligence over any other quality, and he never expected her to wait at home for him while he went out and made a living. He was, as she often says, her biggest booster, pushing her to achievements (law reviews, professorships, the Supreme Court) that Ginsburg herself didn't always think were within reach.

After graduating from Cornell (and spending some time in Fort Sill, Oklahoma, where Martin was stationed during the Korean War), Ginsburg enrolled at Harvard Law School, where she was one of nine women in a class of 500 students. She became the first woman to join the prestigious Harvard Law Review, and after transferring to Columbia Law School to join her husband in New York (the two had a daughter, Jane, whom they wanted to raise together), she graduated tied for first in her class.

Even with her exceptional resume, Ginsburg had trouble finding a job after law school. Law office employers openly discriminated against Jews, women, and mothers; Ginsburg, of course, was all three. Only after Columbia professor Gerald Gunther pulled some strings did she get a job working with federal judge Edmund Palmieri, where she inevitably excelled despite her supposed shortcomings. Although Ginsburg and other women lawyers of the time were aware of the discrimination they faced in the job market and elsewhere, they largely took it as a given. The civil rights movement of the 1950s and '60s, and then the women's movement that got its start a little later, had to change the social climate first to allow the law profession—and the law books—to progress as well.

Ginsburg only became engaged with the women's rights movement when she was a professor (and the first woman with tenure) at Columbia Law School, where several of her students asked her to teach a course on women and the law. She started—and very quickly finished—her research on the subject; in the early 1970s, very few gender cases had been taken to the courts, and the laws and statutes of the United States were filled with precedents that stacked the deck against women. Ginsburg soon set about to change all that.

In 1972, Ginsburg began the Women's Rights Project in conjunction with the American Civil Liberties Union (ACLU). Ginsburg and her fellow ACLU lawyers did not immediately attempt to dismantle every law in the country that gave men and women disparate rights and responsibilities. Instead, she used individual test cases—a woman unable to use her military dependent's allowance for her husband, a man who couldn't use his deceased wife's Social Security benefits to care for their infant child, states that didn't obligate women to serve on juries—to knock down the laws one by one, and to point out the deleterious effects that gender stereotypes have on women *and* men. Men are not always breadwinners, she argued; nor are women always housewives. The law should not impose those conditions on everyday people. Rather, it should allow them to be, as she often said, "free to be you and me." In *Reed v. Reed, Frontiero v. Richardson, Weinberger v. Wiesenfeld*, and the many other cases she argued or wrote briefs for in the '70s, gender classifications were struck down. Although Ginsburg eventually lost the battle for the Equal Rights Amendment to the US Constitution, which would have clearly made the equality of men and women a fundamental right for US citizens, her work in the courts went a long way in establishing equality in the eyes of the law.

President Jimmy Carter recognized Ginsburg's keen sense of justice when he appointed her to the US Court of Appeals for the District of Columbia Circuit in 1980, where she served for twelve years. It was from there that she moved to her best and hardest job: the Supreme Court. President Bill Clinton nominated her as the second woman to the court in 1993, and in recognition of her talent and qualifications for the job, she was confirmed by the Senate 96 votes to three.

As a liberal member of the Supreme Court, Justice Ginsburg consistently calls for an interpretation of the Constitution that regards all people equally before the law. One of her most significant, and personal, court opinions was written for the *United States v. Virginia* case, which for the first time allowed women to be accepted into the prestigious state-sponsored Virginia Military Institute. The case (which was decided 7–1) is often viewed as the culmination of her life's work in making the opportunities that have always been available to men available to women as well.

Not every case ends with Justice Ginsburg in the majority—in fact, in the current conservative court, she has been one of the justices most often on the dissenting side. However, even when she is writing a dissent, her words can be powerful and damning. And, in some cases, they have changed the law of the land. After her dissent written for the *Ledbetter v. Goodyear Tire & Rubber Co.* case, a pay discrimination suit, Congress passed the Lilly Ledbetter Fair Pay Act, which effectively overruled the court's majority opinion and removed the statute of limitations on pay discrimination lawsuits. In other dissenting opinions for *Burwell v. Hobby Lobby Stores, Inc.*, *Wal-Mart Stores, Inc. v. Dukes*, and *Shelby County v. Holder*, among others, she has called Congress's and the court's attention to injustice and discrimination, just as she always has. Justice Ginsburg hopes—as so many do—that those dissents, like the one written for *Ledbetter*, might also become the law of the land one day.

The quotes in this book were compiled from an array of Ginsburg's many public appearances, interviews, and writings as well as from some of the most significant cases she advocated as a lawyer and tried as a justice. You can learn more about these cases in the Milestones section at the end of this book (see page 181), which, arranged by year, also includes other important events in the justice's life.

Justice Ginsburg uses the law not to serve corporations or the government or wealthy contributors, but to preserve what she believes was the founding fathers' true purpose (even if, at the time, they didn't realize it *was* their purpose): to create and maintain a society where all citizens have equal stature before the law. And beyond her advocacy as a lawyer, her Supreme Court opinions, and her transformative effect on the law, Ruth Bader Ginsburg's own remarkable life has proven that women are just as deserving of equality—and notoriety—as men are.

Part I

THE LAW

The Law and the Constitution

I CONSIDER MYSELF an originalist, but let me distinguish another kind. Another kind would say, "Judges do not have the power to make law. That's given to the legislature. And to make sure that the judges are not infusing their own beliefs and ideas into the constitutional text, we have to read it literally. We have to cast our minds back over more than two centuries and try to divine how the founding fathers or the authors of the Fourteenth Amendment . . . would decide that." I say, "That's exactly what I'm doing, but I'm putting those men—and they were all men who wrote the Constitution—with us today." And I know that Thomas Jefferson, who prized equality so much but was himself a slave owner, would applaud how that idea of equality has expanded over the decades.

—*The Aaron Harber Show*

THE FOUNDING FATHERS thought in the natural rights vein. Human rights, in their view, antedated the state (or nation). They were given by Higher Authority. They were not the government's to confer. Rather, the government was to be kept from trampling on them.

—**University of Arkansas at Little Rock School of Law, February 7, 1990**

THE CONSTITUTION WAS a remarkable institution. After all, what it did was it rejected the patriarchal power of kings, and it said that people's fortune in the United States was not going to turn on birth status. Those ideas have tremendous growth potential.

—**American Enterprise Institute, April 19, 1990**

TRYING TO DIVINE what the Framers intended, I must look at that matter two ways. One is what they might have intended immediately for their day, and the other is their larger expectation that the Constitution would govern, as [Justice Benjamin] Cardozo said, not for the passing hour, but for the expanding future.

—**confirmation hearings before the Senate Committee on the Judiciary, July 1993**

IF I WERE in a state ratifying convention, I would propose including explicitly in the Bill of Rights . . . the basic statement in the Declaration of Independence that all persons are equally entitled to fundamental human rights. That's the one guarantee that is central to the Declaration of Independence, the equality guarantee, but is missing from the 1787 Constitution and from the Bill of Rights.

—**American Enterprise Institute, April 19, 1990**

WHAT MAY SEEM constitutional in the abstract may be revealed as unconstitutional when viewed in a specific, contemporary world context—a context that the legislators who passed the law foresaw only dimly, if at all.

—**Paul M. Hebert Law Center, October 24, 1996**

THE LAW EXISTS to govern a society. The law exists in the service of a society. So the experience of the society of course is going to be reflected in the law. If the law is aridly logical, it has nothing to do with the way people live, it's not going to be a successful regime.

—**92nd Street Y, September 26, 2017**

THE WORD THAT is never used in the Constitution is "slavery," but it was the burning problem. And the original Constitution has certain imperfections. One of them is, in the very first article, the slave trade was allowed to continue until the year 1808. . . . Our original Constitution doesn't have any equality provision in it because some humans were held in bondage by other humans. Our Constitution didn't get perfected in that regard until after the Civil War.

—**Annenberg Classroom, December 2006**

IF YOU WERE writing a Constitution today, would you look back to an eighteenth-century model and not consider newer constitutions?

—**Yale Law School, 2013**

THE US CONSTITUTION is nearly 220 years old and contains no express provision opposing discrimination on the basis of gender. Equal protection jurisprudence in the United States involves interpretation of the spare command that governing authorities shall not deny to any person "the equal protection of the laws." Those words, inserted into the US Constitution in 1868, were once interpreted narrowly, but over time, they proved to have growth potential.

> —**University of Cape Town, South Africa,**
> **February 10, 2006**

EVERY MODERN HUMAN rights document has a statement that men and women are equal before the law. Our Constitution doesn't. I would like to see, for the sake of my daughter and my granddaughter and all the daughters who come after, that statement as part of our fundamental instrument of Government.

> —**confirmation hearings before the Senate**
> **Committee on the Judiciary, July 1993**

THE ADOPTION OF the equal rights amendment would relieve the Court's uneasiness in the gray zone between interpretation and amendment of the Constitution. It would remove the historical impediment—the absence of any intention by eighteenth and nineteenth century Constitution makers to deal with gender-based discrimination. It would add to our fundamental instrument of government a principle under which the judiciary may develop the coherent opinion pattern lacking up to now. It also should end the legislative inertia that retards social change by keeping obsolete disciminatory laws on the books.

—*American Bar Association Journal,* **January 1977**

IN THEORY, THE job [of giving men and women equal rights] could be done without an equal rights amendment. But history strongly suggests that the task will continue to be relegated to a legislative backburner without the propelling force supplied by the ERA.

—on the Equal Rights Amendment, *Update on Law-Related Education,* **Spring 1978**

ANY HUMAN RIGHTS guarantee that is phrased in grand, general terms is vulnerable to a scare campaign. That is what's happening to the Equal Rights Amendment. The Equal Rights Amendment is not comparable to the amendment that says eighteen-year-olds can vote. That amendment plainly means eighteen and not seventeen. Because the ERA reads, "Equality under the law shall not be denied or abridged by the United States or by any state on account of sex," people can distort its meaning.

—*Women of Wisdom*, 1981

AN EQUAL RIGHTS Amendment is not a cure-all. It takes people who care about implementing the right to ensure that it becomes real and not just [a] paper statement.

—Yale Law School, 2013

MEASURED MOTIONS SEEM to me right, in the main, for constitutional as well as common law adjudication. Doctrinal limbs too swiftly shaped, experience teaches, may prove unstable.

—**New York University School of Law, March 9, 1993**

IT WOULD BE perverse to interpret the term "Legislature" in the Elections Clause so as to exclude lawmaking by the people, particularly where such lawmaking is intended to check legislators' ability to choose the district lines they run in, thereby advancing the prospect that Members of Congress will in fact be "chosen . . . by the People of the several States."

—**on the Arizona legislature's attempt to remove districting power from a voter-appointed commission, court opinion,** *Arizona State Legislature v. Arizona Independent Redistricting Commission,* **June 29, 2015**

THE LEGISLATURE'S RESPONSIVENESS to the people its members represent is hardly heightened when the representative body can be confident that what it does will not be overturned or modified by the voters themselves.

—on the Arizona legislature's attempt to remove districting power from a voter-appointed commission, court opinion, *Arizona State Legislature v. Arizona Independent Redistricting Commission*, June 29, 2015

WHAT DO I think is enduring? "Congress shall pass no law respecting freedom of speech or of the press." That right to speak your mind and not worry about big brother government coming down on you and telling you the right way to think, speak, and write—that's tremendously important.

—Rathbun Lecture on a Meaningful Life at Stanford University, February 6, 2017

THE SECOND AMENDMENT is outdated in the sense that its function has become obsolete. And, in my view, if the court had properly interpreted the Second Amendment, the court would have said, "That amendment was very important when the nation was new. It gave a qualified right to keep and bear arms, but it was for one purpose only, and that was the purpose of having militiamen who were able to fight to preserve the nation."

—*The Takeaway*, September 15, 2013

YOU CANNOT HAVE a death penalty that's administered with an even hand. That's the problem. Who gets the death penalty? It's a roulette wheel, and that's not a system of justice.

—Smithsonian Associates, February 12, 2015

THE INCIDENCE OF capital punishment has gone down, down, down, so that now I think there are only three states that actually administer the death penalty. Not even whole states, but particular areas of states. It may depend on who is the district attorney. So we may see an end to capital punishment by attrition, as there are fewer and fewer executions.

—**Washington Council of Lawyers Summer Pro Bono and Public Interest Forum, July 24, 2017**

SOME THINGS THAT I would like to change: one is the electoral college. But that would require a constitutional amendment, which is . . . powerfully hard to do.

—**Rathbun Lecture on a Meaningful Life at Stanford University, February 6, 2017**

THE US JUDICIAL system will be the poorer,
I have urged, if we do not both share our
experience with, and learn from, legal systems
with values and a commitment to democracy
similar to our own.

—**International Academy of Comparative Law,
American University, July 30, 2010**

I THINK OUR system is notable for its
transparency. We don't pretend that the law is
always clear and certain. Many times, there's a
good argument to be made on both sides on what
the law is.

—**Duke University School of Law, July 21, 2017**

Lawyers, Judges, and the Practice of Law

MY FIRST EXPOSURE [to the law] was as a college student in the heyday of Senator Joe McCarthy from Wisconsin. There was a huge Red Scare in the country, and this was a senator who saw a Communist in every corner and was hauling people before the Senate investigating committee [and] the House Un-American Activities Committee and drilling them about some organization they had joined in the depths of the Depression. . . . I had a professor for constitutional law who pointed out to me that there were lawyers standing up for these people and reminding our Congress that our Constitution guarantees our right to think, speak, and write as we believe, and not as a big brother government tells us is the right way to think, speak, and write. And we have a Fifth Amendment that protects people against self-incrimination. So I thought that was a pretty nifty thing—a lawyer could make a living, and yet do good for the society in which he lives.

—**Duke University School of Law, July 21, 2017**

IT IS GENERALLY not ideology that keeps lawyers from helping to repair tears in their communities, nation, and world, and in the lives of the poor, the forgotten, the people held back because they are members of disadvantaged or distrusted minorities. It is more likely to be apathy, selfishness, or anxiety that one is already overextended. Those are forces not easy to surmount. Yet lawyers who consider themselves not simply tradesmen working for a day's pay, but members of a true and learned profession, will make the effort to overcome inertia, the workloads on their tables, and the shortness of the day, for the rewards are great.

—**American Bar Association Initiative, May 2, 2006**

A LAWYER'S SKILL is not to dump the kitchen sink before the judge, but to refine the arguments to the ones that a judge can accept.

—**LawProse interview, 2015**

IF YOU'RE GOING to be a lawyer and just practice your profession, well, you have a skill, so you're very much like a plumber. But if you want to be a true professional, you will do something outside yourself, something to repair tears in your community, something to make life a little better for people less fortunate than you.

—**Rathbun Lecture on a Meaningful Life at Stanford University, February 6, 2017**

RECENT COMMENTARY FEATURES studies purporting to show that the legal profession is one of the most unhappy and unhealthy on the face of the earth. But the satisfactions of public service hold the potential to unlock the iron cage that modern practice has become for too many lawyers.

—**Brooklyn Law School, November 16, 2000**

THE SECURITY I feel is shown by the command from Deuteronomy displayed in artworks, in Hebrew letters, on three walls and a table in my chambers. "Zedek, Zedek, tirdof" "Justice, Justice shalt thou pursue," these artworks proclaim; they are ever present reminders of what judges must do "that they may thrive."

—**Touro Synagogue Celebration of the 350th Anniversary of Jews in America, August 22, 2004**

A JUDGE IS bound to decide each case fairly, in accord with the relevant facts and the applicable law. The day a judge is tempted to be guided, instead, by what "the home crowd wants" is the day that judge should resign and pursue other work.

—**answers to the Senate Committee on the Judiciary's confirmation questionnaire, July 1993**

What a judge should take account of is not the weather of the day, but the climate of an era.

—confirmation hearings before the Senate
Committee on the Judiciary, July 1993

CRITICISM OF THE courts, and similarly criticism of other branches of government, should not be resented. Rather, it should be accepted with good grace and considered thoughtfully. For judges who are lifetime appointees, reasoned criticism has a special importance. It helps maintain on the bench healthy attitudes of humility and self-doubt.

—**answers to the Senate Committee on the Judiciary's confirmation questionnaire, July 1993**

JUDGES MUST BE mindful of their place in our constitutional order; they must always remember that we live in a democracy that can be destroyed if judges take it upon themselves to rule as Platonic guardians.

—**confirmation hearings before the Senate Committee on the Judiciary, July 1993**

THAT IS WHY we have the law. That is why we have a system of stare decisis. It keeps judges from infusing their own moral beliefs, from making themselves kings or queens.

—confirmation hearings before the Senate Committee
on the Judiciary, July 1993

LET ME BORROW from a great judge of [the Second] Circuit, Learned Hand, who, in remarks about [Benjamin] Cardozo, stated what makes the good judge. And that is someone who doesn't attempt to win the game by sweeping the opposing chess pieces off the table. He said of Cardozo that he sometimes told the other side's story better than the advocate had. And an honest count—I think that's the most important thing that a judge on any level can give, not to disguise what's really at stake and not to either ignore or distort the points that count in the other direction.

—Second US Circuit Judicial Conference, June 17, 2000

THE EFFECTIVE JUDGE ... strives to persuade, and not to pontificate. She speaks in "a moderate and restrained" voice, engaging in a dialogue with, not a diatribe against, coequal departments of government, state authorities, and even her own colleagues.

—New York University School of Law, March 9, 1993

THE CONTROVERSIES THAT come to the Supreme Court, as the last judicial resort, touch and concern the health and well-being of our nation and its people; they affect the preservation of liberty to ourselves and our posterity. Serving on this Court is the highest honor, the most awesome trust that can be placed in a judge. It means working at my craft—working with and for the law—as a way to keep our society both ordered and free.

—confirmation hearings before the Senate Committee on the Judiciary, July 1993

The Supreme Court

ALL OF US appreciate that the institution we serve is far more important than the particular individuals who compose the Court's bench at any given time. And our job, in my view, is the best work a jurist anywhere could have. Our charge is to pursue justice as best we can.

—**New England Law, March 13, 2009**

THAT'S WHAT WE see as our principal mission: to keep the law of the United States more or less uniform.

—**Rathbun Lecture on a Meaningful Life at Stanford University, February 6, 2017**

IF EVERYBODY AGREES, if all the law courts are in agreement, there's no need for us to step in. But when good judges are of different minds on what is the right answer, that's when we step in, so there will not be one US law on the West Coast, another one in the middle states.

—**Northern Virginia Technology Council, December 17, 2013**

SUPREME COURT JUSTICES are not final because we are infallible, but we are infallible only because we are final.

> —tribute to Chief Justice William Rehnquist,
> October 22, 1995

THE SUPREME COURT, unlike the political branches of government, is a totally reactive institution. As one fine court of appeals judge said, the federal judges don't make the conflagrations. They do what they can to put them out.

> —Rathbun Lecture on a Meaningful Life at
> Stanford University, February 6, 2017

I THINK IF you took a poll today of the three branches of government, which one do the people think is doing the best job, we'd be way out in front of Congress.

> —Duke University School of Law, July 21, 2017

WHAT IS AN activist judge? If you judge it by willingness to strike down laws passed by the political branches, then I would have to say I am probably the most restrained judge currently on the Supreme Court, because this "conservative" court has struck down as unconstitutional too many laws.

—**Brandeis University, January 28, 2016**

WHAT MAKES JUDGES unlike legislators: we don't just say, "I vote that the petitioner should win," or "I vote that the respondent should win." We have to give reasons for every decision we make. Sometimes, in the process of stating your reasons, you begin to say, "Am I right? Did I overlook this question or that question?" And, not often, but sometimes, a justice will say, "This opinion was not right. I was wrong at the conference. I'm going to take the other position."

—**C-SPAN, July 1, 2009**

WHAT HAMILTON SAID was that the judiciary was the least dangerous branch because it possessed neither the purse nor the sword. But it did possess one thing, well, really two: reason and judgment. And you can think of some remarkable times in our country when that really mattered. Think of our Supreme Court and its 1954 decision declaring segregation in our nation's public schools unconstitutional.... Well, the Supreme Court had no troops, but President Eisenhower called them out to make certain that the court's judgment would be followed. And that's the way it has been. There have been some rocky times, yes, but for the most part the Supreme Court's power comes from its reason and its judgment and the recognition of the rest of the system of the value of that institution.

—**Southern Methodist University, February 1, 1998**

ORAL ARGUMENT IS very important. . . . It's the first time since we granted review in the case that all nine of us are thinking about these issues together.

> —National Legal Aid and Defender Association
> Leadership Appreciation Luncheon, June 27, 2014

SOME YEARS AGO, a former law clerk turned law professor . . . ranked Justices by the number of laughs they provoked at oral argument. He rated me, his former boss, the "least funny Justice who talks."

> —American Constitution Society, June 15, 2012

PEOPLE SAY, "Do you miss being an advocate?" And I smile and think, well, I have a very select audience, but I still consider myself an advocate. I would rather carry a court than write a stirring dissent.

> —University of Connecticut School of Law,
> March 12, 2004

I FEEL PRETTY good if I'm the fifth vote that decides the case one way. I feel even better if I'm with four and pick up a fifth vote based on the writing.

—**James Madison High School, July 27, 1994**

THERE'S NO VOTE trading in argument. There's no, if you side with me on this case, I'll side with [you on another case]. Never, that never happens.

—**National Convention for the American Constitution Society for Law and Policy, June 13, 2015**

WILLINGNESS TO ENTERTAIN the position of the other person, readiness to rethink one's own views, are important attitudes on a collegial court. If your colleagues, who are intelligent people and deserve respect, have a different view, perhaps you should then pause and rethink, Am I right? Is there a way that we can come together? Is this a case where it really doesn't matter so much which way the law goes as long as it is clear?

—**confirmation hearings before the Senate Committee on the Judiciary, July 1993**

A JUSTICE, CONTEMPLATING publication of a separate writing, should always ask herself: is this dissent or concurrence really necessary? Consider the extra weight carried by the Court's unanimous opinion in *Brown v. Board of Education*. In that case, all nine justices signed one opinion making it clear that the Constitution does not tolerate legally enforced segregation in our Nation's schools.

—Harvard Club of Washington, DC, December 17, 2009

I WOULD GIVE an interpretation of an intricate provision of the internal revenue code as a classic example of the kind of case where I will say, even though I disagreed, I will bury my dissent—we call that a graveyard dissent—and go along with the majority. But if it's an important question . . . I will go my own way. I will never compromise when it's a question of, say, freedom of speech, press, [or] gender equality.

—Duke University School of Law, July 21, 2017

I think most of my dissents will be the law someday.

—Tanner Lecture on Human Values,
February 6, 2015

Although I appreciate the value of unanimous opinions, I will continue to speak in dissent when important matters are at stake.

—Harvard Club of Washington, DC, December 17, 2009

You're writing [A dissent] for a future age, and your hope is that, with time, the court will see it the way you do.

—Aspen Wye Fellows Discussion, May 24, 2017

What this court produces is an opinion of the court, so you're not writing just for yourself. You're writing, hopefully, for the entire court, but if not, at least for the majority of the members. And you have to take account of what they think.

—C-SPAN, July 1, 2009

I continue to aim for opinions that both get it right and keep it tight, without undue digressions or decorations or distracting denunciations of colleagues who hold different views.

—American Law Institute, May 19, 1994

AGREEMENT IS KIND of boring. Disagreement is more engaging. That's why the press seldom talks about the high level of agreement among all of the justices.

—**American Law Institute, May 23, 2017**

I WOULDN'T SAY it will inevitably divide on party lines. During my now 24 years at the Court, the most "liberal" justices were both . . . registered Republicans themselves: John Paul Stevens and David Souter.

—**Duke University School of Law, July 21, 2017**

CITIZENS UNITED IS probably the most important [recent case], in that the Court had an opportunity to stop making elections turn on who can raise the most money. That opportunity was passed, and . . . I hope someday that decision will be overturned.

—**Thomas Jefferson School of Law's Women and the Law Conference, February 8, 2013**

I FULLY EXPECT that someday we will have campaign finance regulation. I hope it will be in my lifetime, but as each year goes by and we see more and more the pernicious effects of huge campaign drives, I think it's the reality that your contribution is going to give you access to a legislator that you wouldn't have without it.

—University of Minnesota Law School,
September 16, 2014

THE HARDEST CASES for me—they're not necessarily the most complicated legally—are death penalty cases. So those are the cases that I find most trying to be part of, to be the last step between life and death.

—Aspen Wye Fellows Discussion, May 24, 2017

I HAD TO make a hard decision. I could have said, as Justice Brennan and Justice Marshall did, "I'm going to take myself out of this. I'm going to say the death penalty is in all cases unconstitutional, period." But if I did that, I would have no voice in what's going on. I would not be able to make things, perhaps, a little better.

—**University of California Hastings College of Law,
September 15, 2011**

I ASKED SOME people, particularly the academics who said I should have stepped down last year: "Who do you think the president could nominate and get through the current Senate that you would rather see on the court than me?" No one has given me an answer to that question.

—*New Republic*, **September 28, 2014**

I CAN'T IMAGINE what this place would be—I can't imagine what the country would be—with Donald Trump as our president. For the country, it could be four years. For the court, it could be—I don't even want to contemplate that.

—*New York Times*, July 10, 2016

I HAVE IT on reliable authority that reporters would like us to add to our opinions a "practical effects" section in which we spell out the real-world impact of the opinion. But they know that is wishful thinking, for case law generally does not work that way. In our common law system of adjudication, matters seldom can be fully settled "on the basis of one or two cases"; they generally "require a closer working out," often involving responses by, or a continuing dialogue with, other branches of the federal government, the States, or the private sector.

—Loyola University Chicago School of Law,
August 22, 1997

IT IS TRUE, as Jeanne Coyne of Minnesota's Supreme Court famously said: at the end of the day, a wise old man and a wise old woman will reach the same decision. But it is also true that women, like persons of different racial groups and ethnic origins, contribute what the late Fifth Circuit Judge Alvin Rubin described as "a distinctive medley of views influenced by differences in biology, cultural impact, and life experience." Our system of justice is surely richer for the diversity of background and experience of its judges.

—**American Sociological Association
Annual Meeting, August 11, 2006**

Women

and the

Law

IN MY GROWING-UP years and in Justice
O'Connor's, most men of the bench and bar
had what the French call an "idée fixe," the
unyielding conviction that women and lawyering
do not mix. Well, it ain't necessarily so, and
that is revealed in very ancient texts. In Greek
mythology, Pallas Athena was celebrated as the
goddess of reason and justice. To end the cycle of
violence that began with Agamemnon's sacrifice
of his daughter Iphigenia, Athena created a court
of justice to try Orestes, thereby installing the
rule of law instead of the reign of vengeance. And
recall also the biblical Deborah. She was at the
same time prophet, judge, and military leader.
This triple-headed authority was exercised by
only two other Israelites, both men: Moses and
Samuel.

—**Philadelphia Bar Association quarterly
meeting, October 23, 2003**

WHY DID IT take distinguished lawmen so long to open the gates? Tradition was a large factor. For most of our nation's history, the concepts "woman" and "lawyer" were thought incompatible. Until 1920, there was the excuse that citizens who had no vote, no voice in making laws, had no business administering, enforcing, or interpreting them.

—**University of Puget Sound School of Law,
November 2, 1978**

[FLORENCE ALLEN] FINISHED the year second in her class, and her classmates complimented her on her "fine masculine mind," on thinking "just like a man." Allen herself had a different perception. She once said, "When women of intelligence come to recognize their share, their responsibility for the courts, a powerful moral backing will be secured for the administration of justice."

—**on Florence Allen, the first woman to serve
on a state supreme court, National Association of
Women Judges, October 7, 1995**

IN MY GROWING-UP years, there were so many limits on what a girl could aspire to be. She could not be a police officer, she could not be a firefighter, she could not be a coal miner, she could not work at night. There were all these restrictions. There were very few women lawyers, maybe three percent of the bar, and there were even fewer judges. So I never aspired to be a lawyer, certainly not a judge, because if I had to make a living, I had better be a teacher.

—*The Kalb Report*, April 17, 2014

A WIDELY USED property law casebook, in an edition published in 1968, offered this bit of comic relief: "Land, like woman," the text said, "was meant to be possessed." We have come a long way since those now ancient days.

—Foreword, *Yale Journal of Law & Feminism*, 2002

THE FEW WOMEN who braved law school in the 1950s and 1960s, it was generally supposed, presented no real challenge to (or competition for) the men. One distinguished law professor commented at a 1971 Association of American Law Schools meeting, when colleagues expressed misgivings about the rising enrollment of women that coincided with the call up of men for Vietnam War service: Not to worry, he said. "What were women law students after all, only soft men."

—**American Sociological Association Annual Meeting, August 11, 2006**

EMPLOYERS WERE TOTALLY up front in saying, "We don't want any lady lawyers in this shop," or, "We had a woman lawyer once, and she was terrible." So my answer? "How many men have you engaged that didn't work out?"

—**Georgetown University Law Center, September 7, 2016**

I AM FAR from an aggressive person, but I went to law school with nine women in an entering class of 500-odd. . . . We felt that if we were called on in class, we had to get it right, because if we didn't, we would be failing. Not just for ourselves, but the professor would say, "Oh, that's what women law students are like." So we were accustomed to being in the limelight. We took it as kind of our responsibility to teach our male classmates and teachers that women have everything it takes to be successful in the law.

—**Georgetown University Law Center, April 8, 2010**

MY HUSBAND WAS a law school teacher, and when he called for a volunteer, invariably a man's hand would go up. He had a colleague who said, "Don't call on the first hand that's raised. Wait a few seconds, and then there'll be a woman who raises her hand." The idea was a guy would speak off the top of his head, a woman would think before she spoke.

—**European University Institute, February 2, 2016**

SURELY THERE WAS a chill wind for women in the law schools of the 1950s, although many of us barely noticed it while we were there. It was expected, taken for granted. Our sense of injustice was not aroused until years later when younger women, many of them touched deeply by the experiences in the 1960s civil rights movement, said the signpost at the gate was wrong. It should be changed from "Welcome to the Strange and Singular" to "Women are Wanted by the Law Fully as Much as Men Are."

—University of Puget Sound School of Law,
November 2, 1978

WHEN I GRADUATED from Columbia Law School in 1959, not a law firm in the entire city of New York would employ me.... I struck out on three grounds: I was Jewish, a woman, and a mother. The first raised one eyebrow, the second two, the third made me indubitably inadmissible.

—Harvard University, October 7, 1993

[SANDRA DAY O'CONNOR] said, "If Ruth and I came of age in a time when there was no discrimination against women, we would be retired partners in a major law firm."

—*CBS Sunday Morning*, October 9, 2016

AT THE TIME I ... started to teach, you could count on one hand the number of women holding jobs at the professorial level in law schools. There were then no women at the court of appeals level, no women at all.

—C-SPAN, March 28, 1986

WOMEN WEREN'T ON the bench in numbers, on the federal bench, until Jimmy Carter became president. . . . He took a look at the federal judiciary and said, "You know, they all kind of look like me." But that's not how the great United States looks.

—National Convention for the American Constitution Society for Law and Policy, June 13, 2015

THE BREAKTHROUGH ON the United States Supreme Court was the appointment of Justice Sandra Day O'Connor, born and bred a Republican, head of the . . . Arizona senate. But we two voted remarkably alike in every case that involved women's opportunities.

> —**National Museum of Women in the Arts,
> March 16, 2014**

THE ANNOUNCEMENT THE president just made [of my nomination to the Supreme Court] is significant, I believe, because it contributes to the end of the days when women, at least half the talent pool in our society, appear in high places only as one-at-a-time performers.

> —**Supreme Court nomination acceptance speech,
> June 14, 1993**

MY DAUGHTER IS sometimes asked how she feels about her mother's appointment as second woman ever to serve on the Supreme Court. She answers, as I would, "It's fine, but it would be finer still when so many women are judges in all the courts of our land, that no one keeps count anymore."

—**Women's Bar Association of the District of Columbia, May 24, 1994**

THE NATIONAL ASSOCIATION of Women Judges, with great foresight it turns out, had a little celebration at the Court when I took my seat. They presented T-shirts to Sandra and to me. Hers read, *I'm Sandra, not Ruth,* and mine was *I'm Ruth, not Sandra.*

—*O, The Oprah Magazine,* **May 15, 2001**

THERE IS ONE key to Justice O'Connor's opinions and mine that I think you will not find in the run of my colleagues. And that is, we stick to the arguments. We don't waste any words saying something nasty about our colleagues, about the judges in the lower court.

— **National Constitution Center, March 7, 2008**

THE HARDEST TIME for me on the US Supreme Court was when I was all alone, when Justice Sandra Day O'Connor retired. It didn't look right to have one little woman and eight rather well-fed men. The public perception was wrong. But now we are three, we are one-third of the bench.

—**keynote conversation at World Justice Forum V, July 20, 2017**

WOMEN BELONG IN all places where decisions
are being made. I don't say [the split] should be
50-50. It could be 60 percent men, 40 percent
women, or the other way around. It shouldn't be
that women are the exception.

—*USA Today*, May 2009

IN MY LIFETIME, I expect there will be among
federal judicial nominees, based on the
excellence of their qualifications, as many sisters
as brothers in law. That prospect is indeed cause
for hope, and its realization will be cause for
celebration.

—Supreme Court swearing-in ceremony,
August 10, 1993

TODAY ABOUT HALF the nation's law students and more than one-third of our federal judges are women, including three of the justices seated on the United States Supreme Court bench. Women hold more than 30 percent of law school deanships in the United States and serve as general counsel to 24 percent of Fortune 500 companies. In my long life, I have seen great changes.

—*New York Times*, October 1, 2016

WHAT GIVES ME great pleasure is to see women arguing every kind of case that comes before this court. You know, in not-so-ancient days for me, it was thought that women belonged in certain jobs only, particularly in family law, also in tax, rarely as prosecutors, rarely as litigators of any kind. But nowadays, I really could not type the cases in which we tend to have women as advocates. It's not uncommon to have women lawyers arguing both sides, to be opposing counsel, these days.

—Q & A session with eighth graders at the
Supreme Court, May 11, 1994

Sometimes people ask me, "So, now there are three of you. When do you think you will have enough women on the US Supreme Court?" And I think: when we are nine.

—Georgetown University Law Center, September 7, 2016

WOMEN CAN EXCEL in any area of the law that interests them if they are willing to put in the hours of work that it takes to become expert in one area or another. So with no doors being closed, women should choose what they feel . . . that they are best equipped to do.

—**Georgetown University, April 27, 2017**

I AM HEARTENED by a recent University of Michigan survey . . . showing that of all lawyers graduated from that fine law school, women with children are the most content. They are beleaguered, the survey report noted, but they are also satisfied. They enjoy their family lives. They enjoy their jobs. And to the extent each causes stress, each also provides respite from the other.

—**California Women Lawyers, September 22, 1994**

THERE IS . . . one discordant, jarring note—the tendency to regard one's feminism as the only true feminism, to denigrate rather than to appreciate the contributions of others. If that fatal tendency can be controlled, feminist legal theory, already an intellectual enterprise of the first dimension, will indeed be something to celebrate.

—**University of Chicago Legal Forum Symposium, October 1988**

THERE IS A considerable distance yet to travel, but what a long way we have come from the day President Thomas Jefferson told his secretary of state, "The appointment of a woman to public office is an innovation for which the public is not prepared. Nor," Jefferson added, "am I."

—**Women's Bar Association of the District of Columbia, May 24, 1994**

Part II

CIVIL LIBERTIES

Free to Be You and Me

American Rights and Values

I AM THE beneficiary myself of my father being able to leave the Old World where conditions were not good and to come here and make a living and raise a family. That is America to me.

—George Washington University, February 23, 2017

WHAT IS THE difference between a New York City garment district bookkeeper and a Supreme Court justice? Just one generation, my life bears witness, the difference between opportunities open to my mother, a bookkeeper, and those open to me. Where else but in the USA could that happen?

—Touro Synagogue Celebration of the 350th Anniversary of Jews in America, August 22, 2004

HOW CAN I describe the American dream?...
Maybe it's captured by the first ride I took on a
New York subway after returning from several
months in Sweden, where everybody looked the
same. And here I was on the subway, and [there
was] the amazing diversity of the people of the
United States. You know, the motto is "E pluribus
unum," "Of many one," and that's the idea that we,
more than just tolerating, we can appreciate our
differences and yet pull together for the long haul.

—**Academy of Achievement interview, August 17, 2010**

I DON'T JUDGE the past harshly, because they
couldn't perceive things as we do today. But I
hope the main theme of the United States—that
it welcomes all people, respects all religions, all
creeds—that fundamental value will remain and
will flourish.

—**National Press Club, July 10, 2013**

MAINTAINING LIBERTY AND freedom in a time of terror is always difficult, and we have made some dreadful mistakes. Think of what happened to people of Japanese ancestry on the West Coast in World War II. I think we learn from our mistakes; we won't make that mistake again. . . . Of course security is important, but our individual rights must be preserved. Otherwise, we're no different from the forces that we're fighting against.

—University of Colorado Law School,
September 19, 2012

IN BAD TIMES, and in an oppressive society, our humanity should cause us to keep in the front of our minds, not our weakness, but our strength— our strength to hold tight to our human decency so that never, in the service of political leaders, will we administer laws or executive decrees that deny the humanity, the human dignity, of others.

—American Jewish Committee, May 4, 1995

WE MUST NEVER forget the horrors which our brethren were subjected to in Bergen-Belsen and other Nazi concentration camps. Then, too, we must try hard to understand that for righteous people hate and prejudice are neither good occupations nor fit companions.

—**bulletin of the East Midwood Jewish Center,**
June 21, 1946

WE REMEMBER IN sorrow that Hitler's Europe, his Holocaust Kingdom, was not lawless. Indeed, it was a kingdom full of laws, laws deployed by highly educated people—teachers, lawyers, and judges—to facilitate oppression, slavery, and mass murder. We convene to say "Never again," not only to Western history's most unjust regime, but also to a world in which good men and women, abroad and even in the USA, witnessed or knew of the Holocaust Kingdom's crimes against humanity, and let them happen.

—**National Commemoration of the Days of**
Remembrance, April 22, 2004

WHILE THERE IS much light in today's world, there remains in our universe disheartening darkness, inhumanity spawned by ignorance and hate. We see horrific examples in the Middle East, parts of Africa, and Ukraine. . . . With vision and action we can join hands with others of like mind, kindling lights along paths leading out of the terrifying darkness.

—**American Jewish World Service website,
March 18, 2015**

I AM OPTIMISTIC [in the] long run. It was a great man [who] once said that the true symbol of the United States is not the bald eagle; it is the pendulum. And when the pendulum swings too far in one direction, it will go back. Some terrible things have happened in the United States, but one can only hope that we learn from those bad things.

—***BBC Newsnight*, February 23, 2017**

UNLIKE OUR ANCESTORS in their Exodus from Egypt, our way is unlikely to be advanced by miraculous occurrences. In striving to drain dry the waters of prejudice and oppression, we must rely on measures of our own creation—upon the wisdom of our laws and the decency of our institutions, upon our reasoning minds and our feeling hearts. And as a constant spark to carry on, upon our vivid memories of the evils we wish to banish from our world. In our long struggle for a more just world, our memories are among our most powerful resources.

—**National Commemoration of the Days of Remembrance, April 22, 2004**

A GREAT JURIST said the way to fight false facts is by true facts. So when a false fact is stated, the people who care will say, "No, that's not so, that is not the fact. Indeed the fact is—whatever it really is." So I think the best check is people who will call out those who are disseminating falsehoods and criticize them for what they are.

—**University of Hawai'i at Mānoa, February 16, 2017**

I THINK THE press has played a tremendously important role as watchdog over what the government is doing. And that keeps the government from getting too far out of line, because they would be in the limelight. So yes, there are all kinds of excesses in the press too, but we have to put up with that, I think, given the alternative.

—*The Kalb Report*, **April 17, 2014**

THE PROVISION OF health care is today a concern of national dimension, just as the provision of old-age and survivors' benefits was in the 1930s.

—on the Affordable Care Act, concurring opinion,
National Federation of Independent
Business v. Sebelius, **June 28, 2012**

IN THE FULLNESS of time, moreover, today's young and healthy will become society's old and infirm. Viewed over a lifespan, the costs and benefits even out: The young who pay more than their fair share currently will pay less than their fair share when they become senior citizens.

—on the Affordable Care Act, concurring opinion,
*National Federation of Independent Business v.
Sebelius,* June 28, 2012

THERE IS AN overriding interest, I believe, in keeping the courts "out of the business of evaluating the relative merits of differing religious claims," . . . or the sincerity with which an asserted religious belief is held. Indeed, approving some religious claims while deeming others unworthy of accommodation could be "perceived as favoring one religion over another," the very "risk the Establishment Clause was designed to preclude."

—on the Supreme Court's decision to allow corporations
to opt out of birth control coverage on religious grounds,
dissenting opinion, *Burwell v. Hobby Lobby Stores, Inc.,*
June 30, 2014

RELIGIOUS ORGANIZATIONS EXIST to foster the interests of persons subscribing to the same religious faith. Not so of for-profit corporations. Workers who sustain the operations of those corporations commonly are not drawn from one religious community. Indeed, by law, no religion-based criterion can restrict the work force of for-profit corporations.

—on the Supreme Court's decision to allow corporations to opt out of birth control coverage on religious grounds, dissenting opinion, *Burwell v. Hobby Lobby Stores, Inc.,* June 30, 2014

PEOPLE THINK, "WHY bother voting? This is a secure Republican district, or this is a secure Democratic district, so my vote doesn't count." That's not a good thing for democracy.

—on gerrymandering, 92nd Street Y, September 26, 2017

Equal Justice under the Law

A PERSON'S BIRTH status should not enter into the way that person is treated. A person who is born into a certain home with a certain religion or is born of a certain race, those are characteristics irrelevant to what that person can do or contribute to society.

—confirmation hearings before the Senate Committee
on the Judiciary, July 1993

WE HAD JUST fought a war, the Second World War, against an odious form of racism. And yet our troops, through most of the war, were separated by race. Apartheid in America really had to go after the Second World War, because racism of the kind we had in the United States was wholly against what we were fighting for abroad.

—University of California Hastings College of Law,
September 15, 2011

I RECALL ONCE we were coming back from some weekend vacation. We were driving through Pennsylvania, and there was what we would today call a bed and breakfast, with a sign outside that said, "No dogs or Jews allowed." I'd never seen anything like that before. . . . I felt upset, because I was very proud of being born and bred in the USA.

—*Only in America*, September 2, 2004

PEOPLE WHO HAVE known discrimination are bound to be sympathetic to discrimination encountered by others, because they understand how it feels to be exposed to disadvantageous treatment for reasons that have nothing to do with one's ability, or the contributions one can make to society.

—confirmation hearings before the Senate Committee on the Judiciary, July 1993

If we don't protect the people we don't like, we're going to lose protections for ourselves. The Fourth Amendment doesn't say, "You can search the bad guys, but not the good guys."

—Aspen Institute Socrates Program, October 23, 2014

THE COURT TODAY arms the police with a way routinely to dishonor the Fourth Amendment's warrant requirement in drug cases. In lieu of presenting their evidence to a neutral magistrate, police officers may now knock, listen, then break the door down, nevermind that they had ample time to obtain a warrant.

—dissenting opinion, *Kentucky v. King*, May 16, 2011

BIAS BOTH CONSCIOUS and unconscious, reflecting traditional and unexamined habits of thought, keeps up barriers that must come down if equal opportunity and nondiscrimination are ever genuinely to become this country's law and practice.

—dissenting opinion, *Adarand Constructors, Inc. v. Peña*, June 12, 1995

THERE IS A need to look with special suspicion at any law that disadvantages a group of people, especially when those people are not proportionately represented in legislative decision making or executive decision making.

—**Georgetown University, April 27, 2017**

TITLE VII BECAME effective in July 1965. Employers responded to the law by eliminating rules and practices that explicitly barred racial minorities from "white" jobs. But removing overtly race-based job classifications did not usher in genuinely equal opportunity. More subtle—and sometimes unconscious—forms of discrimination replaced once undisguised restrictions.

—**dissenting opinion, *Ricci v. DeStefano*, June 29, 2009**

NOT UNTIL *Loving v. Virginia*, . . . which held unconstitutional Virginia's ban on interracial marriages, could one say with security that the Constitution and this Court would abide no measure "designed to maintain White Supremacy."

—dissenting opinion, ***Adarand Constructors, Inc. v. Peña*, June 12, 1995**

PEOPLE WHO THINK you could wave a magic wand and the legacy of the past will be over are blind. Think of neighborhood living patterns. We still have many neighborhoods that are racially identified. We still have many schools that, even though the days of state-enforced segregation are gone, segregation because of geographical boundaries remains.

—***The Rachel Maddow Show*, February 16, 2015**

SPECIAL CIRCUMSTANCES JUSTIFY vigilant judicial inspection to protect minority voters— circumstances that do not apply to majority voters. A history of exclusion from state politics left racial minorities without clout to extract provisions for fair representation in the lawmaking forum. . . . The equal protection rights of minority voters thus could have remained unrealized absent the judiciary's close surveillance.

—on gerrymandering voting districts to protect minority voters, dissenting opinion, *Miller v. Johnson*, June 29, 1995

"[V]OTING DISCRIMINATION STILL exists; no one doubts that." . . . But the Court today terminates the remedy that proved to be best suited to block that discrimination. The Voting Rights Act of 1965 (VRA) has worked to combat voting discrimination where other remedies had been tried and failed. Particularly effective is the VRA's requirement of federal preclearance for all changes to voting laws in the regions of the country with the most aggravated records of rank discrimination against minority voting rights.

—dissenting opinion, *Shelby County v. Holder*, June 25, 2013

THROWING OUT [FEDERAL] preclearance [of voting laws] when it has worked and is continuing to work to stop discriminatory changes is like throwing away your umbrella in a rainstorm because you are not getting wet.

—dissenting opinion, *Shelby County v. Holder*, June 25, 2013

JUST AS BUILDINGS in California have a greater
need to be earthquake-proofed, places where
there is greater racial polarization in voting
have a greater need for prophylactic measures to
prevent purposeful race discrimination.

—dissenting opinion, *Shelby County v. Holder*,
June 25, 2013

SOME MEMBERS OF the historically favored race
can be hurt by catchup mechanisms designed
to cope with the lingering effects of entrenched
racial subjugation. Court review can ensure that
preferences are not so large as to trammel unduly
upon the opportunities of others or interfere too
harshly with legitimate expectations of persons
in once-preferred groups.

—dissenting opinion, *Adarand Constructors, Inc.
v. Peña*, June 12, 1995

THE STAIN OF generations of racial oppression is still visible in our society, . . . and the determination to hasten its removal remains vital. One can reasonably anticipate, therefore, that colleges and universities will seek to maintain their minority enrollment—and the networks and opportunities thereby opened to minority graduates—whether or not they can do so in full candor through adoption of affirmative action plans. . . . Without recourse to such plans, institutions of higher education may resort to camouflage. . . . If honesty is the best policy, surely Michigan's accurately described, fully disclosed college affirmative action program is preferable to achieving similar numbers through winks, nods, and disguises.

—on the Supreme Court's decision that the University of Michigan's affirmative action policy violated Title VII and the Equal Protection Clause, dissenting opinion, *Gratz v. Bollinger*, June 23, 2003

GOVERNMENT ACTORS, INCLUDING state universities, need not be blind to the lingering effects of "an overtly discriminatory past," the legacy of "centuries of law-sanctioned inequality."... Among constitutionally permissible options, I remain convinced, "those that candidly disclose their consideration of race [are] preferable to those that conceal it."

> **—on the University of Texas's affirmative action policy, dissenting opinion, *Fisher v. University of Texas at Austin*, June 24, 2013**

DURING THE YEARS when gay people hid who they were, there was a kind of discrimination that began to break down very rapidly once they no longer hid in the corner or in the closet.

> **—National Convention for the American Constitution Society for Law and Policy, June 13, 2015**

IT'S NOT AN issue for the young people, at least the ones that I know. It's just not an issue at all. If you love someone and want to marry that person, it should not matter whether it's the same sex or opposite sex.

—**European University Institute, February 2, 2016**

ALL OF THE benefits, all of the incentives that marriage affords would still be available, so you're not taking away anything from heterosexual couples [by allowing homosexual couples to marry]. They would have the very same incentive to marry, all the benefits that come with marriage, that they do now.

—**oral argument, *Obergefell v. Hodges*, April 28, 2015**

MANY PEOPLE, WITH the blessings of Texas, can have sexual relations who are unable to procreate.... Whatever that line might have meant in times gone, it certainly isn't true that sexual relations are for the purpose of procreation, and anything that is not for that purpose is beyond the pale. You can't make that distinction.

—on the Texas law that made consensual same-sex relations illegal, oral argument, *Lawrence v. Texas*, March 26, 2003

I THINK IT will be one more statement that people who love each other and want to live together should be able to enjoy the blessings and the strife in the marriage relationship.

—on officiating a same-sex marriage, *Washington Post*, August 30, 2013

UNDOCUMENTED ALIENS UNFORTUNATELY are not protected by the law, and they are tremendously subject to exploitation. The result is that they are willing to work for a wage that no person who was welcome on our shores would take. I think the answer to that problem is in Congress's lap. People who have been hardworking, taxpaying, those people ought to be given an opportunity to be on a track that leads toward citizenship.

—*The Takeaway*, **September 15, 2013**

"EQUAL JUSTICE UNDER Law" is etched about the US Supreme Court's grand entrance. It is an ideal that remains aspirational. Thanks in part to efforts by lawyers, race, gender, and other incidents of birth no longer bar access to justice as they once did. It remains true, however, that the poor, and even the middle class, encounter financial impediments to a day in court. They do not enjoy the secure access available to those with full purses or political muscle.

—**Washington University School of Law, April 4, 2001**

The History of the Women's Rights Movement

WHEN YOU THINK of the truly great and brave ladies—Susan B. Anthony, Elizabeth Cady Stanton—those were women who didn't have a wave to ride with. We did. We came at a time when society finally was ready to listen.

—New York Bar Association, November 15, 2000

IN 1837 . . . Sara Grimke, noted abolitionist and advocate of equal rights for men and women . . . spoke, not elegantly, but with unmistakable clarity. She said, "I ask no favor for my sex. All I ask of our brethren is that they take their feet off our necks."

—oral argument, *Frontiero v. Richardson*, January 17, 1973

IN THE EARLY 1870s a woman named Virginia Minor said, . . . "I'm a person entitled to the equal protection of the laws. The most fundamental right of a citizen is to vote for the people who will represent her. So, I am a person, I am a citizen, it follows that I have the right to vote." Supreme Court's answer, in that case was, "Of course you are a person. We don't doubt that for a moment. And you are a citizen. But so too are children. And who would think that children should have the right to vote?"

—Aspen Institute Socrates Program, October 23, 2014

THERE WERE WOMEN in front of me and women behind me who made possible the little I was able to accomplish. The women ahead of me were people like Pauli Murray and Dorothy Kenyon. These were feminists in the '40s and the '50s and the '60s. In the hopeless days, they kept the ideas alive.

—Georgetown University Law Center, September 6, 1993

THERE WERE PEOPLE who said . . . "There are other more important things to be done. Women should wait. They should wait until racial injustice is eradicated. They should wait until there's peace in the world." Always that women should wait.

—**New York Bar Association, November 15, 2000**

I THINK THE idea in the 1950s and '60s was that if it was a woman's voice, you could tune out, because she wasn't going to say anything significant. There's much less of that. But it still exists, and it's not a special experience that I've had. I've talked to other women in high places, and they've had the same experience.

—*New York Times*, **July 7, 2009**

I THOUGHT THAT discrimination against women came with the territory and I just had to endure it. I began thinking differently when I was in Sweden in the summers of '62 and '63. And what helped change my thinking was a woman named Eva Moberg who was writing a column in the Stockholm daily paper. And the gist of it was, why should the woman have two jobs and the man only one? Sweden was ahead of the United States, at that point it was well accepted that there should be two earners . . . but the woman was also expected to take the children to the dental checkups, buy the new shoes, have dinner on the table at seven. And there was much discussion among women about this approach—that it wasn't enough that he took out the garbage.

—**Duke University School of Law, January 31, 2005**

BY THE LATE 1960s a revived and burgeoning feminist movement spotlighted the altered life patterns of women. Two factors contributed in particular to this changed atmosphere— the virtual disappearance of food and goods cultivated or produced at home and the access to more effective means of birth control.

—*American Bar Association Journal*, **January 1977**

YOU CAN IMAGINE how exhilarating it was for me when the women's movement came alive in the late '60s, and it became possible to do something about [gender discrimination]. Before that, you were talking to the wind.

—**New York Bar Association, November 15, 2000**

MY STUDENTS, THEY wanted a course in women in the law. And to satisfy that interest I went to the library; in the space of one month I read every federal decision that had ever been written in the area of gender in the law, every law review article. And this, I must tell you, was no mean feat at all, because there was barely anything.

—Duke University School of Law, January 31, 2005

AT THE ACLU Women's Rights Project, which I assisted in launching early in 1972, and in the law school seminars I conducted first at Rutgers [New Jersey's State University], then at Columbia [in New York], work progressed on three fronts: we sought to advance, simultaneously, public understanding, legislative change, and change in judicial doctrine.

—University of Cape Town in South Africa, February 10, 2006

WHEN I WAS a teacher at Rutgers and deciding where I should affiliate, with what group should I affiliate, I picked the ACLU because it's not women's rights, it's people's rights. It's men's rights as well as women. I called it the struggle for equal citizenship stature for men and women. And a number of cases we brought were on behalf of men who were disadvantaged simply because they were men.

—*Charlie Rose*, October 10, 2016

THURGOOD MARSHALL AND his coworkers sought to educate the US Supreme Court, step by step, about the pernicious effects of race discrimination. Similarly, advocates for gender equality sought to inform the court, through a series of cases, about the injustice of laws ordering or reinforcing separate spheres of human activity for men and women.

—Centre for Human Rights, University of Pretoria, South Africa, February 7, 2006

OUR STARTING PLACE was not the same as that of advocates seeking the aid of the courts in the struggle against race discrimination. Judges and legislators in the 1960s, and at least at the start of the 1970s, regarded differential treatment of men and women not as malign, but as operating benignly in women's favor.

—**University of Cape Town, South Africa,**
February 10, 2006

PART OF THE picture, too, are civil rights laws that prohibit discrimination on the basis of race, national origin and religion, but not on the basis of sex. For example, gender isn't listed in the public accommodations title of the Civil Rights Act of 1964. A Congress prepared to end the White Cafe was not yet ready to close down the Men's Grill.

—**on the Equal Rights Amendment,** *Update on*
Law-Related Education, **Spring 1978**

IN ONE SENSE, our mission in the 1970s was easy: the targets were well defined. There was nothing subtle about the way things were. Statute books in the states and nation were riddled with what we then called sex-based differentials.

—**University of Cape Town, South Africa,
February 10, 2006**

IN THE ECONOMIC sphere, women were considered pin-money earners, not the earner who counts. The ramifications of that one was that if a woman—let's take a blue-collar worker— she wants to get health insurance for her family at her plant, she is refused that coverage. She's told, "Only a man can get family coverage. Women can cover themselves, but they can't cover their families."

—*Bloomberg*, **February 12, 2015**

LAWS PRESCRIBED THE maximum number of hours or the time of day women could work, or the minimum wages they could receive; laws barred females from "hazardous" or "inappropriate" occupations (lawyering in the nineteenth century, bartending in the twentieth); remnants of the common-law regime denied to married women rights to hold or manage property, to sue or be sued in their own names, or to get credit from a financial institution (thus protecting them from their own folly or misjudgment). All these prescriptions were premised on the assumption that women could not fend for themselves; they needed a "big brother" to lean on.

—**University of Chicago Legal Forum Symposium,**
October 1988

PRINCETON UNIVERSITY WAS running an exemplary summer program to introduce local elementary school students to math and science in an appealing way.... It was opened to 11- and 12-year-old *boys*. Girls could not be included, the University said, because girls distract boys from their studies.

—*Indiana Law Review*, 1999

GROWING UP IN a society in which virtually all positions of influence and power are held by men, women believe that they belong to the inferior sex.

—joint reply brief, *Frontiero v. Richardson*,
January 12, 1973

ALONG THE WAY, an attitude is instilled insidiously. This attitude is described in a nutshell in graffiti etched in a college library carrel in the early 1950s. The epigram reads, "Study hard, get good grades, get your degree, get married. Have three kids, die, and be buried." From the first line, the sex of the writer is impossible to determine. From the second, her sex is impossible to mistake. To cure the problem felt so acutely by the young woman who wrote those words and so many others like her, the law must stop using sex as a shorthand for functional description. It must deal with the parent, not the mother. With the homemaker, not the housewife. With the surviving spouse, not the widow.

—oral argument, *Kahn v. Shevin*, February 25, 1974

WHERE . . . a wife and husband deviate from the norm—the wife is the family breadwinner, the husband "dependent" in the sense that the wife supplies more than half the support for the marital unit—"benign" legislative judgments serve as constant reminders that, in the view of predominantly or all-male decision-making bodies, life should not be arranged this way.

—joint reply brief, *Frontiero v. Richardson,*
January 12, 1973

THE COMPLAINANT IN *Hoyt [v. Florida]* was a woman charged with killing her husband by assaulting him with a baseball bat, thus terminating an altercation in which she claimed he had insulted and humiliated her to the breaking point. Convicted of second degree murder by an all-male jury, [Gwendolyn] Hoyt had asserted that female peers might better comprehend her state of mind and her defense of temporary insanity.

—on Gwendolyn Hoyt, who unsuccessfully sought
to make jury duty service mandatory for women,
The Supreme Court Review, 1975

WOMEN, AFTER ALL, were the center of home and family life. Therefore, they should not be distracted by being called away from the home for jury duty. So the objective was to let the court understand that these classifications, far from favoring women, kept her, as Justice Brennan said some time in the 1970s, not on a pedestal, but in a cage.

> —on why women were left out of juries,
> Georgetown University, April 27, 2017

A PRIVILEGE TO avoid service at whim, prominently advertised and readily available to any woman or any man, or any other large, stable, distinctive population group, debases the defendant's cross-section right. That right is real only when the obligation to serve is placed on citizens without automatic exemption based solely on their race, national origin, or sex.

> —oral argument, *Duren v. Missouri*, November 1, 1978

THE TWO SEXES are not fungible.... The absence of either may make the jury even less representative of the community than it would be if an economic or a racial group were excluded.

—on the obligation of women to serve in juries, oral argument, *Edwards v. Healy*, October 16, 1974

[THE STRATEGY WAS to] confront the justices with real-life situations so that they could understand that what they once thought was a system of weighing benignly in the woman's favor, in fact disadvantaged them.

—*Washington Post*, May 25, 2014

PEOPLE ASK, WAS it difficult arguing before the Supreme Court in those early '70s? I say, I felt more like a kindergarten teacher than anyone else, because there was knowledge that I had that they didn't have, and I had to try to communicate it in a way they would find appealing.

—Georgetown University, April 27, 2017

I HAD A great secretary at Columbia Law School who was typing my briefs, and she said, "I'm typing these briefs, and all over the word 'sex' is sticking out. Don't you know that the first association of that word is not what you want those judges to be thinking about? So use 'gender.' It's a nice grammar-book term. It will ward off distracting associations."

> —**University of Colorado Law School,**
> **September 19, 2012**

JUSTICE REHNQUIST SAID, "And so, Mrs. Ginsburg, you won't settle for Susan B. Anthony's . . . face on the new dollar coin." . . . I couldn't think of something fast enough. You always think of your best argument in the car going back. So mine would have been, "No, your honor, tokens won't do."

> —**Duke University School of Law, January 31, 2005**

I REMEMBER ONE of my favorite cases, I was arguing it before a three-judge district court in Trenton, New Jersey. And one of the judges commented, "Well, I thought women now have equal opportunity in the military service." And I said, "Well, not yet. Women can't fly planes." And the judge's comment was, "Oh, don't tell me that. Women have always been up in the air. I know from living with my wife and daughter." So, what do you do? You smile and you say, "Yes, your honor, but I know some men who don't have their feet firmly planted on the ground," and go on from there. Not to react in anger, but to take these slights as an occasion, an opportunity to educate the bench.

—**Second US Circuit Judicial Conference,
June 17, 2000**

THE IDAHO STATUTE challenged in *Reed* [*v. Reed*] instructed: As between persons "equally entitled to administer" a decedent's estate, "males must be preferred to females." Sally Reed, whose teenage son died under tragic circumstances, had sought appointment as administrator of his estate. She contested the Idaho courts' determination, under the male-preference statute, to appoint the boy's father (from whom she was divorced), although his application was later in time. The Court moved in a new direction when it ruled, unanimously, that Sally Reed had been denied the equal protection of the laws by the Idaho statute.

—Foreword, *Yale Journal of Law & Feminism*, 2002

SALLY REED'S CASE, it was the turning-point case. It was a unanimous judgment, and it was the first time in history that the Supreme Court ever said a gender line in the law is unconstitutional.

—on *Reed v. Reed*, Georgetown University Law Center,
September 7, 2016

ALL OF THE plaintiffs after that were like
Sally Reed in that they were everyday people.
And what struck me as being great was that
these everyday people thought that the legal
system would rectify the injustice that they had
experienced. There are many nations . . . in the
world where people would think it's hopeless to
expect the courts to strike down a law because it
treats people unfairly.

—**Georgetown University Law Center,
September 7, 2016**

SHARRON FRONTIERO, AN Air Force lieutenant,
sought a housing allowance and health care
for her spouse Joseph, benefits accorded
automatically to a married serviceman, but
denied to a married servicewoman unless she
supplied over three-fourths of the couple's
support. The Frontieros succeeded; the Supreme
Court held the statutory scheme invalid only
insofar as it required a female service member to
prove the dependency of her spouse.

—**on *Frontiero v. Richardson*, Cleveland-Marshall
College of Law, November 9, 1979**

My client, Stephen Wiesenfeld, was determined to rear his infant son personally after his wife's unanticipated death. He sought Social Security benefits as caretaker of a deceased wage earner's child, but he was told he could not even apply. The law provided child-in-care benefits for widowed mothers but not for widowed fathers. The stereotyping was plain: Men were preferred as wage earners, women as caregivers. And the system did not accommodate people who refused to fit into the mold.

—on *Weinberger v. Wiesenfeld, Reason and Passion: Justice Brennan's Enduring Influence*, April 1, 1997

In the decade of the '70s there was one case after another in which gender lines were struck down. Why had that happened? Not because of me. It was because society had changed. Society was moving, and the courts are reactive institutions. They don't lead the way, but they can perhaps accelerate the direction of change.

—Association of Corporate Counsel, September 14, 2016

THE COURT INSTRUCTED Congress and state legislatures: rethink ancient positions on these questions. Should you determine that special treatment for women is warranted, i.e., compensatory legislation because of the sunken-in social and economic bias or disadvantage women encounter, we have left you a corridor in which to move. But your classifications must be refined, adopted for remedial reasons, and not rooted in prejudice about "the way women (or men) are."

—New York University School of Law, March 9, 1993

THE EXPRESSION "WOMEN'S rights" is a bit problematic. It's human rights. It's the rights of all persons to the equal protection of the laws.

—Annenberg Classroom, December 2006

The Rights of Women

IT'S A SADNESS to me that in some places the word "feminism" is considered the "F word." All it means is you think that women should have the same opportunities, that boys and girls should have the same opportunities to use their God-given talent to be whatever they want to and have the ability to be.

—**University of Chicago Law School, May 11, 2013**

I AM FEARFUL, or suspicious, of generalizations about the way women or men are. My life's experience indicates that they cannot guide me reliably in making decisions about particular individuals.

—**National Association of Women Judges District Annual Meeting, September 23, 1984**

AT LEAST IN the law, I have found no natural
superiority or deficiency in either sex. In class
or in grading papers from 1963 until 1980, and
now in reading briefs and listening to arguments
in court for over 17 years, I have detected no
reliable indicator of distinctly male or surely
female thinking—or even penmanship.

> —**Oklahoma Bar Association Women in the Law
> Conference, August 28, 1997**

THE LEADERSHIP STYLE most effective in our
civilized, sophisticated society is not the ruthless
tough guy who forcibly imposes his will on
others. Rather, the qualities that count are the
ability to conciliate among opposing factions
and to foster development of younger, less
experienced people in return for their loyalties.
These qualities do not appear to be linked to one
sex to a greater extent than to the other.

> —**National Association of Women Judges District
> Annual Meeting, September 23, 1984**

Helping raise the level of all women, I think, is something that women should be concerned about.

—University of Chicago Law School,
May 11, 2013

I AM CONCERNED about a threat to women achievers not only from men who are insecure, and whose insecurity causes them to fear women who do not shrink—or pretend to defer—when a male voice speaks. I am concerned too about women, some of them feminists, who seem to have joined the attack by condemning their sisters for taking on "male" values and culture.

—**National Association of Women Judges District Annual Meeting, September 23, 1984**

I ALWAYS THOUGHT that there was nothing an antifeminist would want more than to have women only in women's organizations, in their own little corner empathizing with each other and not touching a man's world. If you're going to change things, you have to be with the people who hold the levers.

—*New York Times*, July 7, 2009

"INHERENT DIFFERENCES" BETWEEN men and women ... remain cause for celebration, but not for denigration of the members of either sex or for artificial constraints on an individual's opportunity. Sex classifications may be used ... to advance full development of the talent and capacities of our Nation's people. But such classifications may not be used, as they once were ... to create or perpetuate the legal, social, and economic inferiority of women.

—court opinion, *United States vs. Virginia*,
June 26, 1996

EVERY GENDER DISCRIMINATION is a two-edged sword. It works both ways.

—oral argument, *Califano v. Goldfarb*, October 5, 1976

I DON'T KNOW of any purely anti-male discrimination. In the end, the women are the ones who end up hurting.

—oral argument, *Califano v. Goldfarb*, October 5, 1976

THE PRIME GENERATOR of discrimination accounted by women in the economic sector is the pervasive attitude, now lacking functional justification, that pairs women with children, men with work.

> —oral argument, *Weinberger v. Wiesenfeld*,
> January 20, 1975

THE QUESTION HAS a certain chicken or egg quality. Should women with household responsibilities be accorded "privileged treatment" to offset this burden until men learn to share it? Or will provision of legal equality and rejection of "privileged treatment" for women hasten the adjustment required of both sexes if each individual is to have the basic right to be considered in terms of his or her own capacities?

> —"The Status of Women," *The American Journal of
> Comparative Law*, October 1, 1972

CONGRESS CAN USE a gender-neutral standard, but it can't simply assume that men are the breadwinners and that women are the dependents.

—oral argument, *Califano v. Goldfarb*, October 5, 1976

THE MORE WE think exclusively of women and children as the natural unit or package, leaving men out of our sight, the more difficult it will be, I fear, for women to achieve fully equal status in all aspects of life and work.

—National Association of Women Judges District Annual Meeting, September 23, 1984

GOVERNMENT SHOULD NOT steer individual decisions concerning household or breadwinning roles by casting the law's weight on the side of (or against) a particular method of ordering private relationships.

—*The Legal Status of Women under Federal Law: Report of Columbia Law School Equal Rights Advocacy Project*, September 1974

STATE ACTORS CONTROLLING gates to opportunity, we have instructed, may not exclude qualified individuals based on "fixed notions concerning the roles and abilities of males and females."

—court opinion, *United States v. Virginia*, June 26, 1996

WHAT IS NECESSARY is a welcome sign, a notice that in the professions, in trades and occupations, women are now as welcome as men. But the notion that they need special favored treatment because they are women, I think, has been what has helped to keep women in a special place and has kept them away from equal opportunity for so long.

—oral argument, *Kahn v. Shevin*, February 25, 1974

GROWING UP, I never saw a woman in a symphony orchestra. Someone came up with the bright idea, let's drop a curtain between the people who are auditioning and the judges. It worked like magic. Almost overnight, women were making their way into symphony orchestras. Now, I wish we could duplicate the dropped curtain in every area, but it isn't that easy.

—Rathbun Lecture on a Meaningful Life at Stanford
University, February 6, 2017

MANAGERS, LIKE ALL humankind, may be prey to biases of which they are unaware. The risk of discrimination is heightened when those managers are predominantly of one sex, and are steeped in a corporate culture that perpetuates gender stereotypes.

—on workplace gender discrimination,
concurring-in-part, dissenting-in-part opinion,
Wal-Mart Stores, Inc. v. Dukes, June 20, 2011

THERE WAS A great case in the 1970s brought by my colleague at Columbia, Harriet Graham. It was against AT&T, and it was about positions for women in middle management. Well, the women did fine on the various tests, up until the last one. And the last one was a total person test. That meant there was an interviewer interviewing the candidate for promotion. And women failed disproportionately at that stage. Why? It wasn't that the interviewer intended to discriminate. It's just that he felt comfortable with someone who looked like himself. He could trust that person. The woman was different. So it's getting past the unconscious bias that exists, still exists, that is a high hurdle to overcome.

> —**Thomas Jefferson School of Law's Women and the Law Conference, February 8, 2013**

WORKPLACE REALITIES FORTIFY my conclusion that harassment by an employee with power to direct subordinates' day-to-day work activities should trigger vicarious employer liability.

> —**dissenting opinion, *Vance v. Ball State University*, June 24, 2013**

IT IS ONLY when the disparity becomes apparent and sizable, *e.g.,* through future raises calculated as a percentage of current salaries, that an employee in Ledbetter's situation is likely to comprehend her plight and, therefore, to complain. Her initial readiness to give her employer the benefit of the doubt should not preclude her from later challenging the then current and continuing payment of a wage depressed on account of her sex.

—on Lilly Ledbetter's right to sue for pay discrimination even after the Title VII time limit, dissenting opinion, *Ledbetter v. Goodyear Tire & Rubber Co.*, May 29, 2007

NEITHER THE GOAL of producing citizen-soldiers nor [the Virginia Military Institute]'s implementing methodology is inherently unsuitable to women. And the school's impressive record in producing leaders has made admission desirable to some women. Nevertheless, Virginia has elected to preserve exclusively for men the advantages and opportunities a VMI education affords.

—court opinion, *United States v. Virginia*, June 26, 1996

PUBLIC UNDERSTANDING HAD advanced so that people could perceive that the [Virginia Military Institute] case was not really about the military. Nor did the Court question the value of single-sex schools. Instead, VMI was about a State that invested heavily in a college designed to produce business and civic leaders, that for generations succeeded admirably in the endeavor, and that strictly limited this unparalleled opportunity to men.

—on *United States v. Virginia*, Wellesley College,
November 13, 1998

DURING THE ERA days, I quoted President Eisenhower, whose comment was, "I am convinced that in the event of another war, women have got to be drafted just like the men." Now, I think that the country has seen, the world has seen, how valuable women can be and how brave they can be.

—Woodrow Wilson International Center for Scholars,
May 21, 2002

USE OF NEUTRAL, strictly job-related criteria for military assignment determinations should assure that no women (and no men) will be forced into positions for which they are unqualified. On the other hand, eliminating sex per se as an assignment determinant will make it possible for women to advance in the military as far as their talents and aspirations permit.

—on the use of gender designations in the military,
The Legal Status of Women under Federal Law: Report of Columbia Law School Equal Rights Advocacy Project,
September 1974

I THINK THAT men and women shoulder to shoulder will work together to make this a better world. . . . Just as I don't think that men are the superior sex, neither do I think women are. I think that it's great that we're beginning to use the talent of all of the people in all walks of life and that we no longer have the closed doors that we once had.

—**Aspen Institute Ideas Festival, July 8, 2010**

WERE I QUEEN, my principal affirmative action plan would have three legs. First, it would promote equal educational opportunity and effective job training for women, so they would not be reduced to dependency on a man or the state. Second, my plan would give men encouragement and incentives to share more evenly with women the joys, responsibilities, worries, upsets, and sometimes tedium of raising children from infancy to adulthood. (This, I admit, is the most challenging part of the plan to make concrete and implement.) Third, the plan would make quality day care available from infancy on. Children in my ideal world would not be women's priorities, they would be human priorities.

—National Association of Women Judges District
Annual Meeting, September 23, 1984

I HAVE NEVER seen a march that was more inspirational.... It was just an uplifting demonstration. It was saying, "We are the people of the United States and we would like to be heard by our government. We would like our government to make laws and policies for the benefit of all the people of the United States."

—on the 2017 Women's March, University of Hawai'i at Mānoa, February 16, 2017

THAT EXPERIENCE, WOMEN of my generation, all of them, have had. When a woman spoke, it was time to tune out. She was not going to say anything very important. But most of that, I think, is gone today.

—University of Colorado Law School, September 19, 2012

THAT HAS BEEN, for me, the most rewarding thing, to see individuals gain a greater sense of self and to see society valuing women—not quite as much as [men]—but we're getting there.

—**Georgetown University Law Center,
September 6, 1993**

MOST PEOPLE IN poverty in the United States and the world over are women and children, women's earnings here and abroad trail the earnings of men with comparable education and experience, our workplaces do not adequately accommodate the demands of childbearing and child rearing, and we have yet to devise effective ways to ward off sexual harassment at work and domestic violence in our homes. I am optimistic, however, that movement toward enlistment of the talent of all who compose "We, the people," will continue.

—*New York Times*, **October 1, 2016**

In 1776 Abigail Adams famously admonished her husband, John, to remember the ladies in the new nation's code of laws. Today, women need not depend on men's memories. In our courts, conference rooms, and classrooms, in ever-increasing numbers, women are speaking for themselves and doing their part, along with *sympathique* brothers-in-law, to help create a better world. Women will of course be remembered, for we are now everywhere.

—**Philadelphia Bar Association quarterly meeting,
October 23, 2003**

Reproductive Rights

OTHER CASES THAT I was involved in from the ground floor were dealing with, I call it the "pregnant problem." Into the early '70s, if a woman taught in public school and she began to show . . . she was put on what was euphemistically called "maternity leave." It was unpaid leave; she had no right to return. . . . And one of the reasons for this policy was, "After all, we don't want the children to think that their teacher swallowed a watermelon."

—University of Colorado Law School,
September 19, 2012

BECAUSE PREGNANCY DISCRIMINATION is inevitably sex discrimination, and because discrimination against women is tightly interwoven with society's beliefs about pregnancy and motherhood, I would hold that [1974 Supreme Court case *Geduldig v.*] *Aiello* was egregiously wrong to declare that discrimination on the basis of pregnancy is not discrimination on the basis of sex.

—dissenting opinion, *Coleman v. Court of Appeals of Maryland*, March 20, 2012

A COMPANY PROVIDES income-replacement payments to temporarily disabled employees for all disabilities that both men and women incur, such as lung cancer, alcoholism and skiing injuries, and all disabilities that only men incur, such as prostatectomies. There is one exception: disabilities arising from pregnancy or childbirth. Is that exclusion sex discrimination? Not at all, ruled the Supreme Court on Dec. 7, 1976, interpreting the Federal law prohibiting job discrimination.

—on *General Electric Company v. Gilbert*, which effectively ruled that pregnancy discrimination did not qualify as sex discrimination and was not covered by Title VII, *New York Times*, January 25, 1977

IF IT IS not sex discrimination to exclude
pregnant women from standard fringe-benefit
programs, is it sex discrimination to fire pregnant
women, refuse to hire them, force them to take
long, unpaid leaves, or strip them of seniority
rights when they return to work?

—*New York Times*, January 25, 1977

WOMEN TEMPORARILY UNABLE to work due
to childbirth or pregnancy-related physical
disability should not be treated as labor force
outcasts. Job security, income protection and
health insurance coverage during such disability
is essential if equal opportunity in the job market
is to become a reality for women.

—*The Legal Status of Women under Federal Law: Report
of Columbia Law School Equal Rights Advocacy Project*,
September 1974

No one is pro-abortion in the sense that they would like to encourage women to get abortions. The question is, if the woman has an unplanned pregnancy, should she have the choice?

—**University of Chicago Law School, May 11, 2013**

One of the reasons, to be frank, that there's not so much pro-choice activity is that young women, including my daughter and my granddaughter, have grown up in a world where they know if they need an abortion, they can get it.

—***Elle*, September 23, 2014**

REPRODUCTIVE CHOICE HAS to be straightened out. There will never be a woman of means without choice anymore. That just seems to me so obvious. The states that had changed their abortion laws before *Roe* [to make abortion legal] are not going to change back. So we have a policy that affects only poor women, and it can never be otherwise, and I don't know why this hasn't been said more often.

—New York Times, July 7, 2009

AN AFRICAN AMERICAN man commented: "We know what you lily-white women are all about. You want to kill black babies." That's how some in the African American community regarded the choice movement. So I think it would be helpful if civil rights groups homed in on the impact of the absence of choice on African American women.

—New Republic, September 28, 2014

IF WE IMAGINE the worst-case scenario, with *Roe v. Wade* overruled, there would remain many states that would not go back to the way it once was. What that means is any woman who has the wherewithal to travel, to take a plane, to take a train to a state that provides access to abortion, that woman will never have a problem. It doesn't matter what Congress or the state legislatures do, there will be other states that provide this facility, and women will have access to it if they can pay for it. Women who can't pay are the *only* women who would be affected.

—*New Republic*, **September 28, 2014**

ROE V. WADE, I should be very clear, I think the result was absolutely right. Texas had the most extreme law in the nation. A woman could not get an abortion unless it was necessary to save her life. Didn't matter that she would be left infirm, whether the conception was the result of rape or incest—none of that mattered. The court could have decided the case before it, which is how the court usually operates. It should have said that law, Texas law, is unconstitutional. . . . There was no need to declare every law in the country addressing abortion, even the most liberal, unconstitutional.

—National Constitution Center, September 6, 2013

WHAT A GREAT organizing tool it is. You have a name, you have a symbol: *Roe v. Wade.* You can aim at that. This decision was made, not in the ordinary democratic process, but by these nine unelected men.

—on why *Roe v. Wade* has incited such strong opposition, University of Chicago Law School, May 11, 2013

YOU READ THE *Roe* opinion, you will never
see the woman standing alone. It's always the
woman in consultation with her physician. So
the picture that I got from that decision was tall
doctor and little woman needing his advice and
care. It wasn't woman centered. It was physician
centered.

—**University of Chicago Law School, May 11, 2013**

YOUR DECISION TO have an abortion is not
necessarily private. It's about your right as a
woman to control your own life's course. . . . You
don't pick that up in *Roe*, that aspect of it.

—**University of Chicago Law School, May 11, 2013**

THE PARTIAL-BIRTH ABORTION Ban Act and the court's defense of it cannot be understood as anything other than an effort to chip away at a right declared again and again by this court and with increasing comprehension of its centrality to women's lives.

—dissent bench announcement, *Gonzales v. Carhart,*
April 18, 2007

THE SOLUTION THE court approves is not to require doctors to inform women adequately of the different [abortion] procedures they might choose and the risks each entails. Instead, the court shields the woman by denying her any choice in the matter—this way of protecting women recalls ancient notions about women's place in society and under the Constitution, ideas that have long since been discredited.

—dissent bench announcement, *Gonzales v. Carhart,*
April 18, 2007

WE HAVE CONSISTENTLY required that laws regulating abortion at any stage of pregnancy and in all cases safeguard not only a woman's existence—her life—but her health as well.

—dissent bench announcement, *Gonzales v. Carhart*, **April 18, 2007**

THE TEXAS LAW called H. B. 2 inevitably will reduce the number of clinics and doctors allowed to provide abortion services. Texas argues that H. B. 2's restrictions are constitutional because they protect the health of women who experience complications from abortions. In truth, "complications from an abortion are both rare and rarely dangerous."

—concurring opinion, *Whole Woman's Health v. Hellerstedt*, **June 27, 2016**

WHEN A STATE severely limits access to safe and legal procedures, women in desperate circumstances may resort to unlicensed rogue practitioners, *faute de mieux*, at great risk to their health and safety.... So long as this Court adheres to *Roe v. Wade* ... and *Planned Parenthood of Southeastern Pa. v. Casey*, ... Targeted Regulation of Abortion Providers laws like H. B. 2 that "do little or nothing for health, but rather strew impediments to abortion,"... cannot survive judicial inspection.

—concurring opinion, *Whole Woman's Health v. Hellerstedt*, June 27, 2016

THE EXEMPTION SOUGHT by Hobby Lobby and Conestoga would override significant interests of the corporations' employees and covered dependents. It would deny legions of women who do not hold their employers' beliefs access to contraceptive coverage that the ACA would otherwise secure.

—on the Supreme Court's decision to allow corporations to opt out of birth control coverage on religious grounds, dissenting opinion, *Burwell v. Hobby Lobby Stores, Inc.*, June 30, 2014

A STATE REGULATION that "has the purpose or effect of placing a substantial obstacle in the path of a woman seeking an abortion of a nonviable fetus" violates the Constitution. . . . Such an obstacle exists if the State stops a woman from choosing the procedure her doctor "reasonably believes will best protect the woman in [the] exercise of [her] constitutional liberty." . . . As stated by Chief Judge Posner, "if a statute burdens constitutional rights and all that can be said on its behalf is that it is the vehicle that legislators have chosen for expressing their hostility to those rights, the burden is undue."

—concurring opinion, *Stenberg v. Carhart*, June 28, 2000

THE REQUIREMENT CARRIES no command that
Hobby Lobby or Conestoga purchase or provide
the contraceptives they find objectionable.
Instead, it calls on the companies covered
by the requirement to direct money into
undifferentiated funds that finance a wide
variety of benefits under comprehensive health
plans. Those plans, in order to comply with
the ACA . . . must offer contraceptive coverage
without cost sharing, just as they must cover an
array of other preventive services.

> —on the Supreme Court's decision to allow
> corporations to opt out of birth control coverage
> on religious grounds, dissenting opinion,
> *Burwell v. Hobby Lobby Stores, Inc.*, June 30, 2014

Part III

A LIFE OF HER OWN

Memories of a Long Life

ONE OF MY . . . fondest memories of growing up was sitting on my mother's lap while she would read to me. I learned to love reading that way.

—children's book reading at United Way in Santa Fe, New Mexico, August 16, 2016

TWO IS MY lucky number. I was the second woman on the Rutgers faculty, before Columbia. Then the second woman, but the first tenured woman, at Columbia. The second woman on the DC Circuit. And the second woman on the US Supreme Court.

—*The Aaron Harber Show*

If I had any talent God could give me, I would be a great diva. But sad for me, I am a monotone. So I sing in only two places: one is the shower, and the other is my dreams.

—Aspen Wye Fellows Discussion,
May 24, 2017

CORNELL [WHERE GINSBURG was an undergraduate] in the early '50s was . . . considered a great school for girls, because there were four men to every woman. It was a strict quota system. That meant the women were ever so much smarter than the boys. But it wasn't the thing to do to show how smart you were. It was much better that you gave the impression that you weren't working at all, that you were a party girl. So I did my studying in various bathrooms on the campus, then [when] I went back to the dormitory I didn't have homework to do.

—**Academy of Achievement interview, July 14, 2016**

THE DEAN [OF Harvard Law School] greeted the women in the first-year class with an invitation to dinner at his home. . . . The dean brought us into his living room and called on each of us to tell him in turn why we were at the Harvard Law School occupying a seat that could be held by a man.

—*Makers*, **February 26, 2013**

THERE WERE MANY indignities one accepted as just part of the scenery, just the way it was. For example, when I was at Harvard Law School, I was on the Law Review and I was sent to check a periodical in Lamont Library.... There was a man at the door, and he said, "You can't come in." "Well, why can't I come in?" "Because you're a female."

—confirmation hearings before the Senate Committee
on the Judiciary, July 1993

THE LAW SCHOOL asked me to submit the financial statement of my father-in-law. Well, at first I was angry. I knew that no man who married would be asked to submit the financial statement of his father-in-law.

—*Only in America*, September 2, 2004

[GERALD GUNTHER] WAS determined to get me a federal clerkship. So he recommended me to a judge who always hired his law clerks from Columbia, and said, "My candidate for you this year is Ruth Bader Ginsburg." And the judge said, "Well, I've looked at her resume. She has a four-year-old daughter. How can I rely on her?" And the great professor said, "Judge Palmieri, give her a chance. If she doesn't work out, there's a man in her class who will step in and take over for her." That's the carrot. The stick: "If you don't give her a chance, I will never recommend another Columbia clerk to you."

—**University of Colorado Law School,**
September 19, 2012

DID I GET equal pay on my appointment at Rutgers in 1963, the very year the Equal Pay Act became the law of the land in the United States? Emphatically "No." The good Dean of the Law School carefully explained about the state university's limited resources, and then added it was only fair to pay me modestly, because my husband had a very good job.

—**Oklahoma Bar Association Women in the Law Conference, August 28, 1997**

IT WAS MY second year at Rutgers. I had a year-to-year contract, and I was pretty sure that if I told them I was pregnant I wouldn't get a contract for the next year. So I wore my mother-in-law's clothes. It was just right, she was one size larger, and I got through the spring semester. When I had the new contract in hand, I told my colleagues when I came back in the fall there would be one more in our family.

—***What It Takes*, September 26, 2016**

I DON'T KNOW how many meetings I attended in the '60s and the '70s, where I would say something, and I thought it was a pretty good idea.... Then somebody else would say exactly what I said. Then people would become alert to it, respond to it.

—USA Today, **May 2009**

I THINK MY work is what saved me through two bouts of cancer.... It was knowing that I had a job to do, an important job, so I couldn't dwell on the aches and pains. I just had to do the job.

—University of Notre Dame, September 12, 2016

THERE IS NOTHING like a cancer bout to make one relish the joys of being alive. It is as though a special, zestful spice seasons my work and days. Each thing I do comes with a heightened appreciation that I am able to do it.

—Women's Health Research Dinner, May 7, 2001

AFTER MY COLON-CANCER surgery, [my husband] Marty said, "You must get a trainer." He said I looked like a survivor of Auschwitz.

—*The New Yorker*, **March 11, 2013**

I HAVE A personal trainer who has been with me since 1999.... [My workout routine] is an hour, and in, oh, about the first segment there are push-ups and something called a plank, and then there are various weights to lift. We do this ... between seven and eight, so I can watch *Newshour*.

—**Virginia Military Institute, February 1, 2017**

YOU KNOW WHAT was copied, for the Notorious RBG? It's the Notorious B.I.G., famous rapper. And when I was told that this was the Tumblr that these two law students had created, I said, well, perfectly understandable. We have one thing in common. You have something in common with Notorious B.I.G.? Of course! We were both born and bred in Brooklyn, New York.

—Rathbun Lecture on a Meaningful Life at Stanford University, February 6, 2017

I DON'T THINK that a justice should have uppermost in her mind, a Democratic president appointed me, so I must leave to be sure that another Democratic president can appoint my successor. I will do this job as long as I feel that I can do it full steam.

—*CBS Sunday Morning*, October 9, 2016

This is the
hardest job
I've ever had.
I go to sleep
thinking
about these
cases, not
about getting
older.

—*Santa Fe New Mexican*, August 23, 2014

I USED TO have an answer [to how long I would stay on the Supreme Court] that worked for a lot of years. It was, "Justice [Louis B.] Brandeis, when he was appointed, he was the same age as I was [when I was appointed]: 60. And he stayed for 23 years, so I expect to stay at least as long." Well, now I have passed Brandeis, I passed [Justice Felix] Frankfurter in my tenure, so my answer is, as long as I can do the job full steam, I will do it.

—**Equal Justice Works, October 27, 2017**

I JUST TRY to do the good job that I have to the best of my ability, and I really don't think about whether I'm inspirational. I just do the best I can.

—*Bloomberg*, **February 12, 2015**

Friends, Family, and Other Influences

My mother died of cancer the day before I was to graduate from James Madison High School in Brooklyn. [My daughter] Jane and I have experienced her ideal of being successful independent women. The woman who taught me to prize learning would be pleased to know that today my granddaughter, Clara, represents the third generation of women in our family to attend Harvard Law School.

—*What I Told My Daughter*, **April 5, 2016**

Growing up, there weren't too many [role models] because women were hardly there, so I had one real and one fictitious role model. The real one was Amelia Earhart. The fictitious one was Nancy Drew.

—Rathbun Lecture on a Meaningful Life at Stanford University, February 6, 2017

MOST OF THE books I read in school were Dick and Jane. And Dick was active, riding a bicycle. Jane was in a pretty party dress, demure. But Nancy Drew was a doer and an actor, and her then-boyfriend mostly did what she told him to do.

—**University of Notre Dame, September 12, 2016**

AT CORNELL UNIVERSITY, professor of European literature Vladimir Nabokov changed the way I read and the way I write. Words could paint pictures, I learned from him. Choosing the right word, and the right word order, he illustrated, could make an enormous difference in conveying an image or an idea.

—*My Own Words*, **October 4, 2016**

MARTY WAS THE first boy, probably the only boy, I had ever known who cared that I had a brain.

—**on husband, Marty Ginsburg, Georgetown University, April 27, 2017**

I had the great good fortune to marry a man who thought my work was as important as his. That was rare in the '50s.

—Yale Law School, 2013

SOME FIRST-YEAR LAW students are totally consumed by the process, by legal education. They're working day and night, and nothing else enters their lives. But for me there was more to life than just attending law school classes. So I attribute my success in law school in large measure to two people: of course my spouse, and the other, baby Jane.

—**University of Notre Dame, September 12, 2016**

[MARTY]'S ALWAYS MADE me feel I was better than I thought myself. And so I started out by being very unsure of, could I do this brief, could I make this oral argument. Until now. Where I am, I look at my colleagues and I say, "It's a hard job, but I can do it at least as well as those guys."

—**Wheaton College, June 8, 1997**

JANE HELPS ME very much to be a whole person, because I do tend to get consumed by my work. And as Jane knows, I could sit at my desk and read my briefs and write my opinions for 20 hours a day if somebody didn't say, "It's time to go to the movies. It's time for you to see your grandchildren, so I'm coming to DC for the weekend." So if my life is sane and if it's full, it's in large measure because I have such a remarkable daughter.

—Women's Bar Association of the District of Columbia, October 27, 1993

MY CHILD [JAMES]—I called him lively, his teachers called him hyperactive. And I could expect a call once a month to tell me about my child's latest escapades, to come down to see the room teacher or the school psychologist or the principal. And one day when I was particularly weary, I was sitting in my office at Columbia Law School, . . . I said, "This child has two parents. Please alternate calls—and it's his father's turn." Well, Marty went down from his office and went to the school, and he faced three stone faces. And what was James's crime? "Your son stole the elevator." And so Marty's response was, "How far could he take it?" Well, I don't know if it was Marty's humor. . . . I suspect it was when the school had to alternate calls. Calls came barely once a semester. And there was no great improvement in my young son's behavior. But I think people were much more reluctant to call a man away from his work than a woman.

—**University of Colorado Law School,
September 19, 2012**

WELL, I WAS the everyday cook. And Marty was the company and weekend cook. And my daughter, who was a fine cook—when she was in high school, maybe about 15, 16, she noticed the enormous difference between Daddy's cooking and Mommy's cooking, and decided that Mommy should be phased out of the kitchen altogether. She shouldn't be cooking every day. And so, we've been living in DC since 1980. I have not cooked a single meal.

—*The Rachel Maddow Show*, **February 16, 2015**

WHO HAS IT all? Man or woman? Well, I think I do if I think of my entire lifespan. I have had it all, but not necessarily at once. So when Marty was a young lawyer climbing up the ladder to become a partner in his law firm, I was the principal caretaker of the home and children. In the 1970s when I began the ACLU Women's Rights Project, Marty was very enthusiastic about the potential for change, and so he was my biggest supporter. And so then the balance was the other way. I think you accommodate each other at different times in your life.

—**University of Notre Dame, September 12, 2016**

JUDGE LEARNED HAND was a brilliant jurist, and I wanted to clerk for him more than anything, even more than for a Supreme Court justice. And my judge, Judge Edmund Palmieri, lived around the corner from Judge Hand, and would drive Judge Hand into work and back. . . . I'd sit in the back of the car, and this great man would say anything that came into his head. He sang songs at the top of his lungs, he used words that I never heard. And I asked him, "Judge Hand, I don't seem to inhibit your speech when you're in this car. Why won't you consider me as a law clerk?" And he said, "Young lady, I am not looking at you."

—*What It Takes*, **September 26, 2016**

WHEN PRESIDENT CLINTON was mulling over his first nomination to the Supreme Court, Justice Scalia was asked, "If you were stranded on a desert island with your new court colleague, who would you prefer: Larry Tribe or Mario Cuomo?" Justice Scalia answered quickly and distinctly, "Ruth Bader Ginsburg." And within days, the president chose me.

—**eulogy at Justice Antonin Scalia's memorial service, March 1, 2016**

ONCE ASKED HOW we could be friends given our disagreement on lots of things, Justice Scalia answered, "I attack ideas. I don't attack people. Some very good people have some very bad ideas, and if you can't separate the two you've got to get another day job. You don't want to be a judge, at least not a judge on a multimember panel."

—**eulogy at Justice Antonin Scalia's memorial service, March 1, 2016**

IT'S GOOD TO have someone who is super intelligent and is able to explain his point of view. It makes you think harder.

> —**on Justice Antonin Scalia,** *CBS Sunday Morning*,
> **October 1, 2017**

IF OUR FRIENDSHIP encourages others to appreciate that some very good people have ideas with which we disagree, and that despite differences, people of goodwill can pull together for the well-being of the institutions we serve and our country, I will be overjoyed, and I am confident Justice Scalia would be too.

> —**Aspen Institute McCloskey Speaker Series,**
> **August 1, 2017**

Life

Lessons

[My mother] said two things: Be a lady. Be independent. "Be a lady" meant don't give way to emotions that sap your energy, like anger. Take a deep breath and speak calmly.

October 9, 2016

WHAT DID SHE mean by be a lady? Well, she didn't mean somebody who serves tea at four in the afternoon. What she meant was, a lady doesn't waste time on unproductive emotions. A lady doesn't snap back in anger. She isn't envious. She is a lady—that is, if an unkind word is spoken, it's as though she didn't hear it.

—**University of Notre Dame, September 12, 2016**

WHAT BEING INDEPENDENT meant: I'm certain my mother hoped that one day I would meet Prince Charming and get married and live happily ever after. But, she said, no matter whether you achieve that or not, be able to fend for yourself. And that was terrific advice.

—**University of Notre Dame, September 12, 2016**

[MARTY'S] MOTHER TOOK me aside and said, "Dear, I would like to tell you the secret of a happy marriage." And the secret was: it helps sometimes to be a little deaf. And with that she handed me a pair of Max earplugs, which are the best earplugs. That advice I followed through 56 years of a wonderful marriage and in every workplace, including my current job.

—on the advice she got on her wedding day, Association of Corporate Counsel, September 14, 2016

WHEN A THOUGHTLESS or unkind word is spoken, best tune out. Reacting in anger or annoyance will not advance one's ability to persuade.

—*My Own Words*, October 4, 2016

MOST OF US have a perspective, most thinking people do, but . . . it's important to disclose one's biases. I'm not trying to brainwash people, but I'm not going to present myself as neutral.

—*Women of Wisdom,* **1981**

THE LABEL LIBERAL or conservative, any—every time I hear that, I think of the great Gilbert and Sullivan song from *Iolanthe.* It goes, "Every gal and every boy that's born alive is either a little liberal or else a little conservative." What do those labels mean? It depends on whose ox is being gored.

—*PBS NewsHour,* **October 10, 2016**

THINK OF YOURSELF . . . as a teacher. So don't react in anger, because that's going to be counterproductive. If you call someone a sexist pig, you've turned him off.

—**Georgetown University, April 27, 2017**

IT'S IMPORTANT TO be a good listener and not to be so attached to your own view that you close your mind to another way.

—92nd Street Y, October 19, 2014

WHILE YOU LIVE, you learn.

—University of Minnesota Law School,
September 16, 2014

MY RESPONSE TO the distortions [in the press and public] is to try to be a teacher in whatever audience I am in, not to feel angry or frustrated, and say, here's an opportunity to try to tell people the way it really is and hope that there will be people in the audience . . . who, when distortions are let out, will answer them constantly and effectively.

—Wheaton College, June 8, 1997

DON'T BE SHY about speaking up. Have company when you do so, so that you're not a lone voice.

—**Association of Corporate Counsel, September 14, 2016**

I BEGAN TO doubt whether I could manage a young child and law school. And my father-in-law gave me some wonderful advice. He said, "Ruth, if you don't want to go to law school, you have the best reason in the world, and no one will think the less of you. But if you really want to become a lawyer, you will stop feeling sorry for yourself and you will find a way to do it." And I have taken that advice at every difficult turn in my life.

—*Only in America*, **September 2, 2004**

IT BOTHERS ME when people say to make it to the top of the tree you have to give up a family. They say, "Look at Kagan, look at Sotomayor." [The two new Justices are not married and have no children.] What happened to O'Connor, who raised three sons, and I have Jane and James?

—*The New Yorker*, **March 11, 2013**

WHEN I WAS a brand-new judge on the DC Circuit, one of my senior colleagues, Judge Tamm, said, "Ruth, I've been at this business a long time, and one thing I'd like to impart to you: do your best job in each case, but when it's over, when the opinion is out, don't look back. Don't worry about things that have passed. Go on to the next case and give it your all."

—**Thomas Jefferson School of Law's Women and the Law Conference, February 8, 2013**

WHEN I HAD colorectal cancer, Sandra had had breast cancer. She had massive surgery; she was in court hearing argument nine days after her surgery. So her advice to me was, "Ruth, you're having chemotherapy; schedule it for Friday so that by Monday you'll be over it, you'll be over the bad effects." That's how she was. Anything that came her way, she would deal with it. She would just do it.

—**Academy of Achievement interview, July 14, 2016**

CHERISH YOUR DAUGHTERS as much as your sons, and teach them both to stand up for what is right, and to be brave, and not be put down. If at first you don't succeed, then you try and try again.

—**PJ Library interview, March 8, 2017**

So often in life, things that you regard as an impediment turn out to be great good fortune.

—*Makers,* February 26, 2013

I would never tear down unless I am sure I have a better building to replace what is being torn down.

—confirmation hearings before the Senate
Committee on the Judiciary, July 1993

WHEN YOU ARE rejected and you deserve better treatment, don't feel sorry for yourself. Just keep trying, keep showing that you have the stuff it takes, and eventually you will prevail.

—visit to Public School 238, where Ginsburg attended,
June 3, 1994

[ART] MAKES LIFE beautiful.

—*Washingtonian*, October 10, 2012

IT TAKES HARD work to make dreams come true, and if you're willing to put in the hard work, you can achieve and aspire.

—children's book reading at United Way in Santa Fe,
New Mexico, August 16, 2016

I HAVE GOTTEN more satisfaction out of things I did for which I was not paid as I did for most of my paying jobs.

—**Georgetown University Law Center,
September 7, 2016**

IF I WERE queen, I would probably have a gap period after high school . . . to do some kind of public service, whether you go into the military or you help teach at a public school. But I think that it would be good for society if we instilled in young people the notion of service to the community.

—**Association of Corporate Counsel, September 14, 2016**

AS YOU PURSUE your paths in life, leave tracks. Just as others have been way pavers for you, so you should aid those who will follow in your way. Do your part to help move society to the place you would like it to be for the health and well-being of generations following your own.

—**baccalaureate address at Brown University,
May 26, 2002**

MILESTONES

1933

- Joan Ruth Bader is born in Brooklyn, New York, on March 15, 1933, to Celia and Nathan Bader.

1950

- Ruth graduates from James Madison High School; her mother dies of cervical cancer the day before her graduation.

1954

- Ruth graduates from Cornell University as the highest-ranking woman in her class. She is also inducted into Phi Beta Kappa.
- Ruth marries Martin (Marty) Ginsburg, whom she met at Cornell.
- Marty, an officer in the ROTC, is called up for active duty and is stationed for two years in Fort Sill, Oklahoma. During this time Ruth works for the Social Security office in Oklahoma, where she is demoted when she becomes pregnant.

1955

- Jane Ginsburg, the Ginsburgs' first child, is born.

1956

- Ginsburg begins attending Harvard Law School, where she is one of nine women students in a class of 500. She becomes the first woman to join the prestigious Harvard Law Review.

- Marty, who is a year ahead of Ruth at Harvard Law School, is diagnosed with testicular cancer. While he undergoes treatment, Ruth arranges for fellow students to take notes for him and help him study; Marty finishes the year with the highest grades of his law school career.

1958

- Marty moves to New York to accept a position at a law firm after graduating from Harvard Law School. Ruth wants to move with him to New York, so she tries to negotiate for a Harvard Law degree even if she finishes her last year at another institution. The law school refuses, and she transfers to Columbia Law School. At Columbia, she becomes the first woman to serve on the Columbia Law Review.

1959

- Ginsburg graduates from Columbia Law School tied for first in her class.

- After being rejected by every law firm she applies to, Ginsburg begins serving as a law clerk in the office of Judge Edmund L. Palmieri of the US District Court for the Southern District of New York.

1961

- Ginsburg becomes a research associate and later the associate director of a study of Swedish civil procedure sponsored by Columbia Law School. She learns Swedish and lives abroad for months at a time to conduct her research. She publishes a book, *Civil Procedure in Sweden*, coauthored with Anders Bruzelius, about her findings. Her time in Sweden, where women appear in numbers in the workforce and are vocal about gender discrimination, influence her developing views on feminism.

1963

- Ginsburg becomes a law professor, mostly teaching civil procedure, at Rutgers Law School in Newark, New Jersey.

1965

- James Ginsburg, the Ginsburgs' second child, is born in the fall. Ginsburg initially conceals her pregnancy from her employers and colleagues at Rutgers Law School, fearing that if they found out her contract would not be renewed.

1970

- Ginsburg cofounds the *Women's Rights Law Reporter*, the first law journal in the country dedicated exclusively to women's rights issues.

1971

- **Reed v. Reed:** Sally Reed had applied to be the administrator of her deceased son's estate, but when her former husband also applied, the state of Idaho granted him privileges she had asked for. In granting her husband these rights, the state cited a statute that said, when choosing administrators, "men must be preferred to women." The Supreme Court hears the *Reed v. Reed* case and, for the first time, applies the Equal Protection Clause of the Fourteenth Amendment to a question of gender. The court strikes down the Idaho statute and grants Sally Reed administrator status, despite the fact that she is a woman. In her first foray in the Supreme Court, Ginsburg writes the brief for the case, writing out Sally Reed's arguments for the Supreme Court to read as it considered the case (Ginsburg does not herself argue a case before the Supreme Court for two more years). The *Reed* decision is a significant turning point for the court, and Ginsburg uses the case's precedent to argue against gender discrimination throughout the 1970s.

1972

- Ginsburg helps found the Women's Rights Project with the American Civil Liberties Union (ACLU). Throughout the 1970s, the Women's Rights Project brings a number of gender discrimination cases to court in order to establish gender equality throughout the country. Ginsburg is chief litigator for the project. She represents or writes briefs for many of the most significant gender discrimination cases that came to US courts in the 1970s.

- Ginsburg joins the editorial board of the *American Bar Association Journal.*

- Ginsburg becomes a professor at Columbia Law School, where she is the first tenured woman on the faculty.

- Ginsburg joins with other woman petitioners on the faculty of Columbia Law School to file a class-action lawsuit against their employer; they demand (and win) equal pay, pension benefits, and pregnancy coverage.

- Ginsburg represents the maids employed by Columbia when many of them face termination due to budget cuts. (None of the men on the housekeeping staff were due to be fired because of these cuts.) In the end, no maids are fired.

- Ginsburg agrees to represent Susan Struck, a member of the Air Force, on behalf of the ACLU. Struck had become pregnant while serving in the Air Force; the military then had a policy of requiring women to either abort their babies or withdraw from the service. Struck did not want either option. She used only the military leave available to her for the pregnancy and birth, and then returned to the service. Even though she had given the baby up for adoption and used no additional time to give birth, the Air Force still wanted to discharge her. Ginsburg had hoped the case would be the first step in arguing for, and winning, reproductive rights before the Supreme Court. Ginsburg submitted a petition for the case and months later the Supreme Court agreed to hear it. However, the night before the legal team was to submit its brief, the Air Force withdrew Struck's discharge, rendering the case moot. Ginsburg views Struck's case as a missed opportunity to argue that reproductive rights are an issue of gender discrimination (after all, men in the military were not discharged if they had a child) instead of an issue of privacy (which *Roe v. Wade* later turned it into).

- **Moritz v. Commissioner of Internal Revenue:** Charles Moritz, an unmarried man taking care of his elderly mother, wanted to claim a tax deduction that was available for women or married men taking care of dependents but not single men. In the only case they take on together, both Ruth and Marty Ginsburg (a prominent tax lawyer) represent Moritz before the US Court of Appeals for the Tenth Circuit. The court concludes that the tax break violates due process and requires the scrutiny demanded by the *Reed v. Reed* precedent.

1973

- **Frontiero v. Richardson:** A woman in the military, Sharron Frontiero, had wanted to receive a dependent's allowance for her husband. However, the allowance was available only for wives of military members and for any husbands who provided less than half the couple's income. In the first case that she argues before the Supreme Court, Ginsburg explains that the military statute concerning dependents' allowances unfairly discriminates against women as wage earners, violating the Fifth Amendment's Due Process Clause. The Supreme Court agrees with Ginsburg and decides the sex-based classification in the military's policy requires a strict standard of review to discover and eliminate gender discrimination.

1974

- **Kahn v. Shevin:** Mel Kahn had applied for and was denied a property tax exemption that was available to widows but not widowers. Ginsburg represents Kahn before the Supreme Court in the case but loses. (It is the only case she loses before the court.) The Supreme Court's opinion states that widows face greater hardship than widowers after the death of their husbands and are therefore in greater need of the tax break than their male counterparts.

- **Edwards v. Healy:** The state of Louisiana had made jury duty optional for women. Ginsburg represents Marsha Healy and a number of other plaintiffs (men as well as women) before the Supreme Court to argue that doing so diminishes the citizenship rights of half the state's population. The Supreme Court vacates the decision of the District Court for the Eastern District of Louisiana, which had upheld the jury duty law, and remands it to that court.

- Ginsburg joins the national board of directors for the ACLU, a post she holds until 1980.

1975

- **Weinberger v. Wiesenfeld:** A widower, Stephen Wiesenfeld, had wished to collect Social Security benefits to support his son after the death of his wife in childbirth. As a widower, he had been denied benefits that would be available to a widow. Ginsburg brings the case before the Supreme Court, in part to demonstrate to the court and public that gender discrimination affects men as well as women. The court rules that the gender discrimination in the Social Security code indeed discriminates against three parties: the deceased wife, the surviving husband, and the baby.

1976

- **Craig v. Boren:** Curtis Craig and a licensed alcohol vendor challenge an Oklahoma law that set the drinking age for men higher than the drinking age for women. Ginsburg submits an amicus brief for the case. (She describes the plaintiffs, a group of fraternity brothers, as the "thirsty boys.") The Supreme Court declares the Oklahoma statute to be unconstitutional and decides that gender-based classifications in the law would henceforward be subject to "intermediate scrutiny."

- **Califano v. Goldfarb:** A widower, Leon Goldfarb, had applied for and was denied Social Security survivor's benefits after his wife's death. To be eligible, his wife would have needed to provide over half his financial support before his death; the same criterion did not apply to widows after their husbands' deaths. Ginsburg argues before the Supreme Court that the

gender-based criterion violates the Due Process
Clause of the Fifth Amendment. The court affirms
that the Social Security statute is discriminatory and
renders it unconstitutional.

1977

- Ginsburg is appointed a fellow at the Center for Advanced Study in the Behavioral Sciences at Stanford University in California, and serves until 1978.

1978

- Ginsburg begins serving on the Council of the American Law Institute.

1979

- Ginsburg joins the board and executive committee of the American Bar Foundation.

- **Duren v. Missouri:** Billy Duren, indicted for first-degree murder and first-degree robbery, had asked that he be tried by a jury composed of a fair cross section of his peers. In Missouri at that time, women could opt out of jury service; accordingly, very few women served on juries. In the last case she brings before the Supreme Court, Ginsburg argues on behalf of Duren, saying that allowing women to opt out of juries implies that they are less essential members of a fully functioning social system. The court rules that the exclusion of women from juries violates the Constitution's fair cross-section requirement for juries and remands the case back to trial court.

1980

- President Jimmy Carter appoints Ginsburg to the US Court of Appeals for the District of Columbia Circuit. As a district court judge, Ginsburg follows a mostly moderate path, seeking agreement with the two other judges of the three-member panel whenever possible.

1982

- The Equal Rights Amendment, which would have made the equality of men and women a constitutional right, falls three states short of ratification. Ginsburg had long been—and continues to be—a strong advocate for the ERA, arguing that the US law system, like so many others throughout the world, ought to give gender equality a strong constitutional basis.

1993

- President Bill Clinton appoints Ginsburg to the Supreme Court in June, and she is confirmed in August by the Senate with 96 votes to three.

1994

- Along with Justice Scalia, a fellow lover of opera, Ginsburg makes an appearance as an extra in the Washington Opera's production of *Ariadne auf Naxos*.

1995

- **Adarand Constructors, Inc. v. Peña:** The US Department of Transportation had selected a minority-owned subcontractor (Peña) over a non-minority-owned subcontractor (Adarand Constructors), even though the latter had made a higher bid for a contract. The Supreme Court decides that the Department of Transportation had violated the Due Process Clause of the Fifth Amendment by using race as a consideration in awarding the contract to Peña over Adarand Constructors. Ginsburg dissents, writing that Congress has given government entities like the Department of Transportation the right to correct racial injustices through affirmative action—so that, in some cases, it may be appropriate to prefer a minority candidate on the basis of race.

- **Miller v. Johnson:** In order to ensure a fair representation of black voters, the state of Georgia had gerrymandered a voting district to ensure that it would have a majority of black voters. The Supreme Court determines that the district was so bizarrely formed that it did not fairly represent a community of voters. In her dissenting opinion, Ginsburg writes that the voting district should not be thrown out just because it appears to be illogically formed, and she argues that it is sometimes right for the judiciary to intervene in districting cases when issues of racial discrimination are in question.

1996

- **United States v. Virginia:** The US government brought a case against prestigious state-sponsored Virginia Military Institute demanding that it accept women applicants. The state had no equivalent school for women, thus denying them the academic and professional opportunities it gave so many men. Ginsburg writes an opinion for the court that allows qualified women applicants access to the school for the first time. The opinion is often viewed as the culmination of her career fighting for the equality of men and women in the eyes of the law.

- **M.L.B. v. S.L.J.:** A mother (M.L.B.) was barred from appealing for parental rights because she was unable to pay the fee required to prepare her record. The Supreme Court rules that the parent's inability to pay the fee should not keep her from having her parental rights reviewed. Ginsburg writes the majority opinion.

1997

- Ginsburg administers the oath of office to Vice President Al Gore at the presidential swearing-in ceremony.

- Ginsburg receives the first Sophia Smith Award from Smith College in recognition of her contributions to women's rights.

1999

- **Olmstead v. L.C.:** Two women with mental disabilities had been cleared to live in a community setting under the terms of the Americans with Disabilities Act, but the state of Georgia had required them to remain in an institutional environment because of financial and other considerations. Ginsburg writes the opinion for the Supreme Court, judging that, if they are able, individuals with mental disabilities have a right under the ADA to live in community, despite the state's financial constraints. The decision is significant because it officially determines that individuals with mental as well as physical disabilities are subject to the rights and privileges of the ADA.

- Ginsburg receives the Thurgood Marshall Award from the American Bar Association. She is the first woman to be given the award, which recognizes an individual's contributions to civil liberties and human rights.

- Ginsburg is diagnosed with colorectal cancer, which is successfully operated on in September. She does not miss a day in court, but Marty urges her to begin seeing her trainer, Bryant Johnson, after the cancer bout.

2000

- **Stenberg v. Carhart:** Nebraska had passed a law prohibiting partial-birth abortions unless the procedure saved the woman's life. Leroy Carhart, a doctor who administered abortions, argued that the law placed an undue burden on both himself and his patients. The Supreme Court rules the ban to be unconstitutional. Ginsburg writes a concurring opinion.

- The New York City Bar creates the annual Justice Ruth Bader Ginsburg Lecture on Women and the Law in recognition of Ginsburg's many accomplishments. Speakers have included Gloria Steinem, Justice Elena Kagan, Madeleine Albright, and other groundbreaking women.

- **Bush v. Gore:** The state of Florida's contested votes would determine who won the presidency, and the Florida Supreme Court had ordered a statewide manual recount in order to find the legitimate winner. The Supreme Court hears oral argument on December 11 and issues its opinion December 12 (the electoral college had to meet December 18), a breakneck and highly unusual turnaround rate for the court. The court's opinion opts to stay the Florida Supreme Court's recount, effectively declaring George W. Bush the winner of the presidential election. Ginsburg issues a dissent stating that the US Supreme Court ought to honor the Florida Supreme Court's interpretation of its own statutes and let the recount continue.

2002

- In October, Ginsburg is inducted into the National Women's Hall of Fame.

2003

- **Gratz v. Bollinger:** A lawsuit had been made against the University of Michigan for preferring minority applicants over Caucasian applicants. The Supreme Court's majority opinion decides that the university's admissions policy violated equal protection standards by admitting nearly every minority applicant. Ginsburg dissents, writing that, because the university didn't try to decrease enrollment by certain groups or save seats for others, it was not in violation of equal protection standards.

- **Lawrence v. Texas:** The case challenged a Texas statute forbidding consensual sexual activity between same-sex couples. In a landmark decision, the Supreme Court determines that the statute violates the Due Process Clause. Ginsburg joins in the majority opinion.

- Justices Ginsburg and Breyer make cameos as themselves in the Washington Opera's performance of *Die Fledermaus*.

- Ginsburg receives the Justice Joan Dempsey Klein Honoree of the Year Award from the National Association of Women Judges.

2006

- Justice Sandra Day O'Connor retires from the Supreme Court, making Ginsburg the only sitting woman justice. Ginsburg frequently says that Justice O'Connor's retirement has been the most significant change to the court in her own tenure as a justice.

2007

- **Gonzales v. Carhart:** Leroy Carhart and other doctors who performed abortions had sued to prevent President Bush's Partial-Birth Abortion Ban Act from taking effect, arguing that it placed an undue burden on women and their doctors and would prohibit abortion procedures like dilation and evacuation even if they weren't explicitly included under the act. The Supreme Court majority upholds the act and argues that it would not apply to any abortion procedures beyond its ken. Ginsburg dissents, citing the *Roe v. Wade* and *Casey v. Pennsylvania* precedents and decrying the court's outright hostility to abortion rights.

- **Ledbetter v. Goodyear Tire & Rubber Co.:** Lilly Ledbetter had sued her employers at Goodyear for paying her less than her male counterparts. The Supreme Court's majority opinion denies Lilly Ledbetter's claims for pay compensation, citing the limitations period of Title VII. According to the court, Ledbetter had simply sued too late. Ginsburg's dissent argues that Lilly Ledbetter could not have known about the pay disparity early enough to make a case in court, and that, even if she had known about the unequal pay earlier on, her employer could have simply said that she deserved less pay than her male colleagues. It was only after Ledbetter had proven again and again her worth as an employee and still received less money than her male counterparts that a suit could have held up in court—and at that time, according to the limitation period, it would have been too late. Ginsburg closes her dissent with a call to Congress to correct cases like Lilly Ledbetter's.

2008

- Ginsburg receives the Janet Reno Torchbearer Award from the Women's Bar Association.

2009

- President Barack Obama signs the Lilly Ledbetter Fair Pay Act, his first piece of legislation signed in office. Under the act, every paycheck resets the 180-day deadline in which an employee can make pay discrimination claims under Title VII.

- Ginsburg has surgery to operate on pancreatic cancer in February. Again, she does not miss a day in court.

- **Ricci v. DeStefano:** The case concerns the New Haven fire department's testing and hiring practices; fearing Title VII litigation, the city had thrown out test results because the results appeared racially skewed. (Black and Hispanic firefighters taking the test had failed in overwhelmingly high numbers.) A number of white firefighters and one Hispanic firefighter argued that the city had discriminated against them on the basis of race when it threw out their results. The Supreme Court agrees with the group of white firefighters. Ginsburg, however, dissents, arguing that New Haven had good cause for throwing out the results, and that the Civil Rights Act of 1964 (which the plaintiffs had used to defend their case) was only intended to be used for situations that had *imposed*, and not *corrected*, racial inequity.

- Sonia Sotomayor is confirmed to the Supreme Court in August, bringing the number of women on the court back to two.

2010

- **Citizens United v. FEC:** Citizens United, a conservative nonprofit, argued that the Bipartisan Campaign Reform Act, which regulated "big money" campaign contributions, violated the First Amendment. The Supreme Court agrees with the nonprofit and removes limits from corporate donations to political campaigns. Ginsburg files a dissenting opinion and later says that *Citizens United* is the most regrettable decision of the current court, as the decision has had far-reaching consequences on the ability of corporations to influence politicians.

- Ginsburg receives the Benjamin Nathan Cardozo Memorial Award, given in honor of outstanding American citizens.

- Ginsburg receives an honorary doctorate of law from Princeton University.

- Marty Ginsburg passes away in June. The couple had been married for 56 years.

- Elena Kagan is confirmed to the Supreme Court. Ginsburg says that having three women on the court shows that they are there to stay.

- Ginsburg receives the ABA medal from the American Bar Association.

2011

- **Kentucky v. King:** Police officers in Lexington, Kentucky, had entered a suspect's home without a warrant because they smelled marijuana on the premises and feared he was destroying evidence. The Supreme Court rules that the police had not created the circumstances that caused them to enter the apartment and therefore had not violated the Fourth Amendment. Ginsburg dissents and expresses fear about the precedent the decision would set in other Fourth Amendment cases.

- Ginsburg receives an honorary degree from Harvard University. Harvard Law School, after denying her petition for a degree when she was still a student there, had repeatedly offered her one in the years since she left. Marty always told her to hold out for an honorary degree from the university itself.

- **Wal-Mart Stores, Inc. v. Dukes:** In the largest class-action lawsuit in US history, Betty Dukes and the women employees of Wal-Mart sued their employer for discriminatory pay practices. The Supreme Court's majority opinion, authored by Justice Scalia, states that such a large group of plaintiffs (estimated to be 1.5 million women) could not all possibly file a pay discrimination lawsuit on the same grounds. Ginsburg concurs in part and dissents in part, arguing that discrimination by managers was demonstrably uniform throughout the company and may have been subject to scrutiny under the Federal Rule of Civil Procedure.

2012

- **Coleman v. Court of Appeals of Maryland:** Daniel Coleman, a former Maryland Court of Appeals employee, argued that he had been unlawfully terminated for requesting sick leave for a documented medical issue. He made his claim on the basis of the self-care provision of the Family and Medical Leave Act, which was intended to counter instances of sex discrimination by mandating equal self-care leave for men and women. The Supreme Court's majority opinion states that Coleman was not wrongfully terminated. Ginsburg dissents, upholding the ability of the FMLA to alleviate gender discrimination while also providing equal allowances for men.

- **National Federation of Independent Business v. Sebelius:** Florida and 12 other states had challenged Congress's constitutional right to enact the Affordable Care Act, which leveraged a tax penalty on any individuals without health care and overhauled the insurance market. The Supreme Court upholds the federal government's authority to pass the Affordable Care Act under the Taxing and Spending Clause. In her separate concurring opinion, Ginsburg writes that Congress has the authority to enact the Affordable Care Act under the Commerce Clause, as insurance is something that is bought and sold.

- *Glamour* names the justice one of its women of the year.

2013

- The Association of American Law Schools creates the Ruth Bader Ginsburg Lifetime Achievement Award, which honors distinguished women in the legal community. Ginsburg is the first recipient of the award.

- **Fisher v. University of Texas at Austin:** Abigail Fisher, a white student, argued that the University of Texas had violated the equal protection clause of the Fourteenth Amendment by considering race as a factor in admissions. The Supreme Court states in its majority opinion that race may be considered as a factor in college admissions, but only after strict judicial scrutiny finds that no factor other than consideration of race can achieve the university's diversity goals. Ginsburg dissents, stating that the Equal Protection Clause does not prohibit the consideration of race when it is being used to correct for a history of discrimination.

- **Vance v. Ball State University:** An African American employee of Ball State University, Maetta Vance, had sued her employer because of harassment she experienced from a coworker. The Supreme Court's opinion states that the university is only liable for discriminatory actions committed by a supervisor, not a coworker. In her dissent, Ginsburg argues that a supervisor should be redefined as any colleague with the power to direct an employee's work. She states that the court's opinion ignores the realities of the modern workplace, in which direct supervisors are not the only ones who may affect the daily operations and well-being of an employee.

- **Shelby County v. Holder:** The Voting Rights Act of 1965 called for enhanced scrutiny in counties where racial bias had occurred in the past. Shelby County, Alabama (which had a history of racial discrimination at the polls), argued that that section of the Voting Rights Act was unconstitutional and should no longer be enforced. The Supreme Court concurs with Shelby County, claiming that incidents of race-based discrimination had taken place 40 years ago and are now out of date. In an impassioned dissent, Ginsburg argues that Congress, not the court, has the power to dismantle parts of the Voting Rights Act, and that "second-generation" challenges to voting rights still persist and must be scrutinized.

- NYU law student Shana Knizhnik creates the Notorious R.B.G. Tumblr after researching the *Shelby County v. Holder* case and Ginsburg's rousing dissent. The Tumblr sets off the new internet-driven wave of admiration for the octogenarian Supreme Court justice.

- Ginsburg officiates the wedding of Michael Kaiser and John Roberts. While it is common for Supreme Court justices to preside over weddings, she is the first to officiate a same-sex marriage.

2014

- Ginsburg receives the Rita C. Davidson Award from the Maryland State Bar Association.

- **Burwell v. Hobby Lobby Stores, Inc.:** The owners of Hobby Lobby sought under the Religious Freedom

Restoration Act to deny their employees contraception coverage without incurring the tax penalties of the Affordable Care Act. The Supreme Court majority allows that closely held corporations with sincere religious beliefs are not required to fund birth control coverage in their health insurance plans. In a fiery dissent, Ginsburg writes that the sincere beliefs of a company's owners should not affect the reproductive rights of employees, nor should they counteract the provisions of the Affordable Care Act.

- Ginsburg receives the inaugural Justice John Paul Stevens Lifetime Achievement Award.

- Ginsburg is diagnosed with a blockage in her right artery after experiencing tightness and discomfort during her regular exercise routine. A stent is placed in her right coronary artery to relieve the pressure.

2015

- Ginsburg receives the Radcliffe Medal from the Radcliffe Institute for Advanced Study at Harvard. The award is given in recognition of individuals who have changed society for the better.

- **Obergefell v. Hodges:** Groups of same-sex couples from across the country argued that their states' bans on same-sex marriage violated the Equal Protection Clause and the Due Process Clause. The Supreme Court grants same-sex couples the right to marry throughout the country. Ginsburg joins in the majority opinion.

- **Arizona State Legislature v. Arizona Independent Redistricting Commission:** The Arizona state legislature had questioned the right of a voter-appointed commission to draw district voting lines in the state. Ginsburg and the four other justices in the majority allow that voters have the right to appoint their own commission to determine voting districts and patterns.

- The opera *Scalia/Ginsburg*, written by Derrick Wang, premieres at Castleton Festival. The opera pits the legal theories of the respective justices against each other in a plot based on *The Magic Flute*. Ginsburg, a lifelong fan of the form, is an outspoken champion of *Scalia/Ginsburg*.

- Ginsburg receives the Franklin D. Roosevelt Four Freedoms Award from the Roosevelt Institute.

- The book *Notorious RBG: The Life and Times of Ruth Bader Ginsburg*, based on the Notorious R.B.G. Tumblr, is released.

- *Time* includes Ginsburg in its list of 100 most influential people, with a tribute written by Justice Scalia.

2016

- Ginsburg delivers a eulogy for Justice Scalia at his memorial service in March. The two were longtime friends despite their stark legal differences.

- Ginsburg receives the American Bar Association Rule of Law Award for her efforts in educating domestic and international communities about the law.

- Scientists at the Cleveland Museum of Natural History name a species of praying mantis *llomantis ginsburgae* because its neck plate resembles the justice's iconic jabot, the lacy collar she wears with her robes to court.

- **Whole Woman's Health v. Hellerstedt:** The state of Texas had passed several provisions raising the standards for abortion facilities (which would effectively close many facilities and limit access to abortion). The Supreme Court strikes down the regulations, ruling that they place a substantial burden on women seeking an abortion. Ginsburg writes in a concurring opinion that abortion facilities are overwhelmingly safe for women and that any law limiting access to them would fail under judicial scrutiny.

- In July, Ginsburg criticizes presidential candidate Donald Trump, expressing fear about what he would do to the country and the court if he were elected president. Her comments stir controversy among politicians and the media, and she issues an apology several days after making them.

- Debbie Levy publishes the children's book *I Dissent: Ruth Bader Ginsburg Makes Her Mark*, which sets Ginsburg up as a role model for children.

- In collaboration with Mary Hartnett and Wendy Williams, Ginsburg publishes *My Own Words*, a collection of her best speeches and writings.

- **Sessions v. Morales-Santana:** Luis Ramon Morales-Santana had claimed that he should have derivative citizenship in the United States because of his father, who could have provided derivative citizenship as a mother but not as a father. Morales-Santana argued that the less stringent standards for women violated the Equal Protection Clause. Ginsburg writes the majority opinion for the Supreme Court, which effectively agrees with Morales-Santana's argument but says that it is the job of Congress, not the courts, to correct this error in the law.

- Ginsburg plays the Duchess of Krakenthorp in the opening-night production of *The Daughter of the Regiment* at the Kennedy Center.

2017

- The film based on the 1972 *Moritz* case, *On the Basis of Sex*, begins filming with Felicity Jones as Ruth and Armie Hammer as Marty Ginsburg.

- **Trump v. International Refugee Assistance Project:** President Donald Trump's Executive Order No. 13780, Protecting the Nation From Foreign Terrorist Entry Into the United States, had banned entry into the country from six Muslim-majority countries for 90 days. Several lower federal courts had issued injunctions against enforcing the ban. The Supreme Court cancels its oral argument on the case and issues an unsigned opinion that allows the federal government to stay several of the injunctions.